Literat

Polity's *Why It Matters* series

In these short and lively books, world-leading thinkers make the case for the importance of their subjects and aim to inspire a new generation of students.

Helen Beebee & Michael Rush, *Philosophy*
Robert Eaglestone, *Literature*
Lynn Hunt, *History*
Tim Ingold, *Anthropology*
Neville Morley, *Classics*
Alexander B. Murphy, *Geography*
Geoffrey K. Pullum, *Linguistics*
Graham Ward, *Theology and Religion*

Robert Eaglestone

—————

Literature

Why It Matters

polity

First published in 2019 by Polity Press

Polity Press
65 Bridge Street
Cambridge CB2 1UR, UK

Polity Press
101 Station Landing
Suite 300
Medford, MA 02155, USA

ISBN-13: 978-1-5095-3231-5
ISBN-13: 978-1-5095-3232-2 (pb)

A catalogue record for this book is available from the British Library.

Library of Congress Cataloging-in-Publication Data

Names: Eaglestone, Robert, 1968- author.
Title: Literature : why it matters / Robert Eaglestone.
Description: Cambridge, UK ; Medford, MA : Polity, 2019. | Includes
    bibliographical references and index.
Identifiers: LCCN 2018032457 (print) | LCCN 2018051798 (ebook) | ISBN
    9781509532346 (Epub) | ISBN 9781509532315 (hardback) | ISBN
    9781509532322 (pb)
Subjects: LCSH: Literature--History and criticism.
Classification: LCC PN86 (ebook) | LCC PN86 .E24 2019 (print) | DDC
    801/.3--dc23
LC record available at https://lccn.loc.gov/2018032457

Typeset in 11 on 15 Sabon by Servis Filmsetting Ltd, Stockport, Cheshire
Printed and bound in Great Britain by CPI Group (UK) Ltd, Croydon

For further information on Polity, visit our website: politybooks.com

Contents

v

Acknowledgements

Thanks to: Barbara Bleiman, Poppy Corbett, Pie and Mel Corbett, Jane Davis, Philip Davis, Sarah Dobson, Justin Dyer, Alex Eaglestone, Bella Eaglestone, Ben Knights, Simon Kovesi, Ellen MacDonald-Kramer, Gail Marshall and Pascal Porcheron.

1

What is Literature?

Hello. Excuse me. Can you tell me where I am?
[She waves]
In our country, this is the way we say hello
It is a diagram of movement between two people
It is a sweep on the dial
. . .
Hello. Excuse me. Can you tell me where I am?[1]

This welcome is from the American experimental artist Laurie Anderson; it's a poem, but also a song and a sort of performance (the poet waves her forearm like the sweep of a dial). Is it literature?

No one really knows. We have a kind of hazy and indistinct idea of what literature is, but as soon as we try to pin it down, to define it, literature seems to slip away.

For example, take the idea that literature is simply 'made up' or fiction. But what about writing based on the historical record? Hilary Mantel's historical novels draw on real events; many contemporary playwrights use the exact wording of interviews or government reports for 'verbatim' plays. More, the root of the word *fiction* doesn't just mean untrue: it comes from the Latin word *fingere*, meaning 'to shape, fashion, form'. Every writer – a scientist recording an experiment, a politician composing a speech, a copywriter drafting instructions about how to use a phone – shapes and chooses their words. And if literature tells us about the most important aspects of ourselves, about how we really are, or what, say, being in love is like, are these things untrue if in a poem or novel?

Or take the idea that literature tells a story, uses narrative. On the one hand, there are countless texts we think of as literary that don't use narrative: lyric poems don't tell stories; David Markson's novel *This is Not a Novel* (2001) is made up of a series of statements, for example. On the other hand, there are texts we don't think of as literature which do use narrative: an account of scientific research is a narrative. Telling a story isn't unique to novels, so can't define literature. Perhaps literature is just writing? Not necessarily, if we include, say, a poet making a crying noise or performing a gesture, or we think of the role of silence on stage; there are also 'graphic novels' which combine text and pictures; and some computer games are often so like novels they are called 'ludo-fiction'. And again, writing covers more than literature. There's also the idea that literature means just 'great writing' ('Literature with a capital L'). But, as I discuss later, what makes a work of literature 'great', a 'must-read' for 'every educated person' (part of the 'literary canon'), turns out to be pretty contentious and far from obvious; and a bad poem is still a poem.

Turning to history doesn't help much with a definition either. The word 'literature' came to be used in English in the fourteenth century to mean 'knowing about books' in general. Isaac Newton's works, from the late seventeenth century, were called literature, although we'd call them science today; the same is true of works of philosophy, history, and so on. It was in the mid-eighteenth century that people began to classify writing according to different types, and only then that 'literature' acquired our current vague sense of it as novels, poems and plays. As usual, the categories we use to define things, from grammatical terms to animal species, come much later than the things themselves.

Definition means limit: that's the origin of the word, from the Latin *finis*, with the sense of end, finite, finish. But literature seems unlimited, infinite and, because each work provokes a response – delight, excitement, fascination, boredom, anger – somehow it's always unfinished business. For literature, the categories we generally use just don't seem to work. There are always exceptions, hard cases or examples that don't fit.

And there's a further problem. When you read, you never encounter 'literature' in the abstract: you encounter a particular text, ideally one that grabs you, a novel by J. K. Rowling or Leo Tolstoy, or a poem by Rupi Kaur or Sylvia Plath. It's easier to explain why a particular work of literature matters to you (you identify with the main character or their situation, maybe, or perhaps your mum read it to you when you were a kid); it's harder to explain why 'literature in general' should matter. This is why some provocative people say that literature (meaning, 'literature in general') doesn't even exist.

So right at the beginning of a book called, rather grandly, *Literature: Why It Matters*, we find ourselves a bit lost ('Excuse me. Can you tell me where I am?'). How can we know why literature matters when we don't have more than a hazy sense of what it might be?

I think that wanting to define literature is to approach this question in the wrong way. It is to use the methods of a scientist classifying nature

or a lawyer who demands a cut-and-dried definition of everything. These approaches miss exactly
what's important. In his work the *Poetics*, the
ancient Greek philosopher Aristotle says that the
origin of poetry is representation or imitation (the
Greek word is *mimesis*) and it comes 'naturally to
human beings from childhood': we love to imitate
and we naturally take 'pleasure in representations'
(20). Much of the *Poetics* is like a 'how to' guide
for writing poetry and drama. The Greeks had very
different ideas about literature from us, but we can
take Aristotle's point that literature is not an inert
thing but an action or a craft that we *do*. Literature
is more like a verb than a noun. Enjoying a walk
is different from following the map of its route;
appreciating the flowers of the hedgerow is not the
same as knowing their formal botanical names. The
enjoyment and appreciation may be hard to define
but are real.

So I want to use a different and more sympathetic approach than that of the scientist or lawyer
to think about why literature matters: a way that
tries to express the walk, rather than be the map,
that focuses on the appreciation not the dried
specimens behind glass. This approach isn't less
precise: rather, as legal language frames the law
or mathematical notation describes the movement

of atoms, I'm going to choose a way that best fits the subject it addresses. In order to explore what literature is and why it matters, I'm going to use a literary technique known to everyone who has ever read a story or poem. I'm going to propose a *metaphor* for literature, then explore what it means and its consequences: a kind of *literary critical* analysis. Metaphors – as I'll discuss in detail in chapter 2 – are the tools of thought. So when a poet writes, for example, that 'my love is a rose', it leads to the thought that the love is beautiful (like a rose) but also that it will fade and decay over time (as, like any flower, the rose dies). Inspired by the Laurie Anderson poem I began with ('a diagram of movement between two people'), here's my metaphor: *literature is a living conversation.* And using this metaphor, we can begin to see why literature matters.

This metaphor underlies lots of accounts of literature. Here's Hector, the far-from-straightforward English teacher from Alan Bennett's well-known play *The History Boys* (2004). He say that the

> best moments in reading are when you come across something – a thought, a feeling, a way of looking at things – which you had thought special and particular to you. Now here it is, set down by someone else, a person you have never met, someone even

multiple meanings conveyed

who is long dead. And it is as if a hand has come out
and taken yours.[2]

I'll come back to this later, but it shows one key
obvious aspect of the idea that literature is a living
conversation, that *literature is a communication*.
We often think of communication as simply the
transfer of data from one point another, but much
more is implied by it. Communication needs at
least two people ('a hand has come out and taken
yours'), a language and a medium (books, signs,
lights, vibrations of sound in air, even looks). We
can't even understand 'hello' without finding out
about these: just as every tiny piece of data tells us
a great deal about the people, society and world it
comes from, so even the smallest piece of literature
relies on and somehow manifests a whole world.

Just as a conversation you hold with your friends
can be about anything, so too *literature can be about
anything*. As I've said, this is one of the reasons it
can't be defined. It can be about other people, and
tell you more about an individual than you could
ever really know; it can be about whole societies
and cultures. It can shock or provoke or amaze or
amuse or reform or corrupt you. Literature can be
about the things that matter: beginning and birth,
lies and truth, good and bad, ending and death. But

7

it's also about things that don't matter or don't even exist: mythical people, unicorns, mermaids.

Indeed, *literature* makes *things matter*. This is one of its mysteries. Prince Hamlet looks in wonder at the actor who is crying over the death of the mythical Queen Hecuba and the ruin of the city of Troy: 'What is Hecuba to him, or he to Hecuba, that he should weep for her?'[3] Similarly, a discussion of Dobbie the House Elf makes a generation of readers tear up. Thinking of literature as a conversation helps us explore this. In a conversation we 'bring a subject up' or 'bring to light issues' that concern us or mean something to us, and in doing this we show our own selves. Sometimes, in conversation with others (or even, silently, with ourselves), we discover what we didn't know before, or reframe what we already somehow knew, in order to talk about it. Literature does the same: like conversation, it reveals, brings things up, puts events, experiences and thoughts into language so as to give them meaning.

But this process of revealing isn't shapeless. We talk about 'making conversation' because we make, we shape, what we say. We do this not just in the content of the words we choose but also, for example, in the tone we take: the form. We can say 'hello' angrily, kindly, lovingly, sarcastically, and so on. In conversation, *how* we say something is as important as *what* we say. This is even more powerfully true for literature: the form is as important as – or even more important than – the content. *Form has meaning*: learning about literature is learning about form. Simple examples: an epic, whether it's *Paradise Lost* or *Game of Thrones*, shows its importance by being very (very) long; in contrast, a sonnet shows its sophistication, its control and style in its brevity. The leading British critic Terry Eagleton makes these two points – about how literature makes meaning and the nature of form – when he writes luminously that poetry is 'concerned not just with the meaning of experience, but with the experience of meaning'.[4]

Talking with someone is a creative act: conversation is a kind of improvisation between people, after all. So using the metaphor of literature as a living conversation means that *creativity* exists not just in the work of literature, or in the head of a famous author, but also in us, the reader. The creativity of literature is shared precisely because literature is an activity. This is where Hector's beautiful image, above, is flawed: a hand reaches out in reading, yes, but you have to reach out to take it. This means that literature isn't just about the books on the shelf: it's about you thinking, responding, writing about, *talking with* the books too; and that dialogue can involve multiple speakers, arguing, discussing, thinking, a shared conversation, not just 'a diagram of movement between two people' but one between many. More, this creativity is not confined to lessons or libraries: we use and respond to 'literary techniques' – figures of speech, metaphors, suspense, stories – all the time in our everyday life. Perhaps the very first things we create as infants are speeches and stories – as Aristotle suggests, imitation comes naturally to us – and so just as we are experts in conversation, we are always already experts in creating, responding to, listening to and judging literature. This means that literature is not something magical or cut off from everyday life: it doesn't, or shouldn't (whatever people say), exist on a pedestal.

Just like a conversation, your creative response to literature draws on your mind, heart, feelings, your past and your hopes for the future. But, of course, you change over time, and as you change so the literature which speaks to you changes. The preface to the wonderful novel *The Golden Notebook* (1962) by the Nobel laureate Doris Lessing is one of the best things written about literature and reading: in it she says, 'Remember that the book which bores you when you are twenty or thirty will open doors

10

for you when you are forty or fifty – and vice-versa. Don't read a book out of its right time for you.'[5] As a living conversation, our relationship to a book changes: reading is a *process*. We respond to a book and a book also responds to us. Reading and learning about literature is a sort of 'becoming attuned', just as an instrument shapes a piece of music and a piece of music shapes the instrument. This means, of course, that knowing about literature means something different from just knowing facts about, say, the dates of an author, what happens in chapter 3 or reading the Wikipedia summary. Knowing about a work of literature is about experiencing it as a process, not – although it can sometimes feel like this – as a collection of answers for a quiz or exam: literature's the walk not the map. Knowing the chemical make-up of water is not the same as knowing what it's like to get soaked in a sudden summer storm.

In a normal conversation we often say: 'Please can we talk about this . . . ?'; 'I've lost track, why are we discussing that . . . ?'; 'When I said this, I meant. . . .' A crucial part of a conversation, particularly a long one, is its ability to reflect on and comment on itself. Literature *reflects* on itself too. One of the most famous examples of this comes from George Eliot's novel *Middlemarch* (1871–2). (The writer Virginia

Woolf described it, rightly, as a 'magnificent book which with all its imperfections is one of the few English novels written for grown-up people'.[6]) The narrator tells us that a mirror is 'minutely and multitudinously scratched in all directions', but that if you put a candle up to it 'the scratches will seem to arrange themselves in a fine series of concentric circles round that little sun'.[7] The candle 'produces the flattering illusion of concentric arrangement' and is, she writes, a 'parable' of how we engage with events and other people in the world: we see them illuminated and arranged in relation to us only through our own self-centred concerns. This is one of the themes of *Middlemarch* – the limitations of the characters' (and so our own) interests; but it is also a 'parable' about the book itself, telling us how it wants to be read, as different characters' lives and perceptions illuminate the interwoven web of events. What are mundane events for some are momentous for others, depending on the light of their own candle. Most great works – some critics say all works – have these kind of moments, in which they tell you how they want to be read and understood. This isn't simply a modern invention. There is an amazing moment in Book VIII of Homer's *Odyssey* when Odysseus, the hero of the poem, in disguise, hears a poet sing about him and his comrades: he covers his head with a cloak and cries. We, the audience, see the impact of the poem on the protagonist, and on ourselves, as it connects with experience.

Conversations *exist in time*: they come from what was said before, they happen now, and they shape your future. The same is true with works of literature, which are not, as passionate enthusiasts sometimes suggest, timeless but 'time-full'. Perhaps the most significant sense of this is simply the past context or period of a literary work. In the George Eliot example above, I described a 'mirror' with scratches. What she actually wrote in her parable was a 'pier-glass or extensive surface of polished steel made to be rubbed by a housemaid' set in the context of a scientific experiment about optics: an almost unrecognizable object (who uses a mirror of polished steel now?) located in a different network of social relationships (who has a housemaid?). Similarly, in all of Shakespeare's plays we can find his fears about civil war, the profound concern of his time. Critics interested in the original context of works are often called *historicist* critics. (I'll introduce their notional opposite, *formalist* critics, in the next chapter.)

Literature's rootedness in its past exists, too, through the idea of literary influence. Writers often trace a 'family tree' of works that have influenced them as they modify and reshape stories, themes, language, forms and anything else they choose. (But watch out – writers often don't tell the truth about who has influenced them!) James Joyce's novel *Ulysses* (1922) takes Homer's epic story of the hero Odysseus and transmutes it to his own contemporary Ireland and so changes both what we think a hero is, and what an epic is. This 'family tree' of literary influence is also rooted in the past through genre. Genre just means type: revenge tragedies, love poems, detective stories. Texts often respond or reply to their generic forebears, and this makes the metaphor of literature as conversation especially clear. In the genre of detective fiction, Arthur Conan Doyle's Sherlock Holmes is tall, dynamic, lean, strong, masculine. In response, from the next generation, Agatha Christie's Miss Marple is a meek-seeming old woman who often (on purpose) fades into the background; she is a response (or even a rebuke, perhaps) to Holmes. In contrast, the American writer August Derleth created Solar Pons, a character almost exactly like Holmes (Pons lives at 7b Praed St, not 221b Baker St; his friend is Dr Parker, not Dr Watson; his brother is Bancroft not Mycroft). This is fine (literature can be about anything), but do you want, in a conversation, to hear the same sentence over and over again? Sometimes this idea of a 'family tree' is inflated to cover a tradition or a national idea: we speak of English Literature, Kenyan Literature, Japanese Literature, and so on. But, just as a conversation can go on over times and spaces, so literature doesn't belong within one limited national boundary or time. It exists in a 'nonstandard space and time'.[8] The conversation can flow where it will and we might watch closely those who seem keen to delimit it.

If a work of literature has a past, it also has a present. Writers respond, consciously and unconsciously, to the world they find themselves in; theatre, TV and film directors adapt plays to address current concerns; and you, as a reader, like the candle in the 'pier-glass', cannot but see what you read in relation to yourself. Any text, even from long ages past or far away, exists in the context of the present, and you are already literature's present: you've already begun. Speak to it. It is by speaking to it that the future of literature will come into being. Creative responses lie with writers, sure, but also with readers, adapters, listeners, talkers, preservers, teachers, and so on. You don't know where a literary text might go or lead.

Ideally, a real conversation is *free*. It isn't stilted or anxious, isn't made up of commands or instructions, isn't a tedious explanation or isn't using language to deceive or exert power. An ideal conversation is where everyone can speak; this is achieved less often than it should be. Yet when we speak with someone, we are, in some way, proclaiming our equality with our interlocutor. So not only can literature be about anything and be impossible to define, but it should also be a conversation between equals in which you are free to say anything. This relationship to free-dom has some consequences. One which especially applies to students and teachers is highlighted by Doris Lessing (again): she argues that there 'is only one way to read, which is to browse in libraries and bookshops, picking up books that attract you, reading only those, dropping them when they bore you, skipping the parts that drag – and never, never reading anything because you feel you ought, or because it is part of a trend or a movement'.[9] As a professional teacher of literature, I feel a little conflicted about this obviously right advice: my students clearly *ought* to read the books we plan to read together, but I'm also aware that forcing someone to read a novel or a poem can change that experience, as I discuss later.

But there are also some wider consequences of this freedom: the profound connection between literature and how we live and share the world

16

What is Literature?

[handwritten: Freedom to crititise — form new thoughts — cause rebellion.]

together, politics. The impossibility of limiting the range or form of the literary is why totalitarian rulers ban literature and why writers (and readers) are so often persecuted. Salman Rushdie wrote that the 'creative process is rather like the processes of a free society. Many attitudes, many views of the world jostle and conflict within the artist, and from these frictions the spark, the work of art, is born. This inner multiplicity is frequently very difficult for the artist to bear, let alone explain.'[10] If this is true for writers in the conversation of literature, it is true, too, for readers. The Polish Nobel laureate Czesław Miłosz wrote that poetry reminds us

How difficult it is to remain just one person, *[handwritten: > constantly effected by new ideas,]*
For our house is open, there are no keys in the
   doors
And invisible guests come in and out at will.[11]

This is close to, but a little different from, the idea *[handwritten: > sends a message on our author on to work.]* that all literature is political. George Orwell came to the conclusion that all art, all literature, was a sort of propaganda, a political tool; in contrast, the French writer Maurice Blanchot suggested that literature cannot compete with politics in terms of politics. Both are right, paradoxically: literature is a bit like a secret conversation passed in whispers, just to you; but at the same time, it's a bit like a

17

political speech, something in public, shared, talked about, argued over. Again, this simultaneous duality is part of why it can't be defined. And it's certainly true that the freedom of literature to say anything anyhow, to be both private and public at the same time, makes tyrants and totalitarians, who want to control our public and private worlds, feel uneasy with writers and with readers.

But we ought to be careful. If literature is like a living conversation, then it has the same political problems or risks as a conversation. We know we can exclude people, offend them, refuse to listen to them, ignore them, only hear what we want to hear. If conversation is alive, we can deaden it. A proper conversation is an open conversation between equals, and if literature is a conversation, we have to make sure that it is not exclusive. I wonder: what would it mean not to be involved in, to be cut off from, this conversation? Or only to be able to have the simplest conversation? And: what might it mean to cut yourself off from this conversation? (I have a look at this in chapter 3.) Ironically, one way of cutting people out of the conversation is to put literature on a pedestal, to over-praise it. I mentioned the 'literary canon' earlier, the idea that there is a list of books that everyone should read. Roughly speaking, the canon is one of the most contentious

issues in literature because it is where the idea of
literary value ('This book is great!') and the shaping
power of politics ('You should be like this!') come
together in a kind of command ('Everyone should
read this book in order to be like this!'). In this
context, the trouble is that there is no neutral position from which to judge literary value (you can't
suddenly 'step outside' society to judge a text) and
that the grounds for inclusion or exclusion in the
canon are politicized and not always transparent.
Texts by women, for example, or by authors from
other countries, can often disappear. More, the 'list
of great books' establishes itself in a kind of inertia
and is enforced by people's expectations ('we've
always read this') and often economics (a school
can't buy hundreds of new books to teach, so trots
out the same ones; most publishers won't bring out
a book that won't sell). One way of dealing with
the literary canon, however, comes from the idea
of literature as a living conversation. Alan Bennett's
English teacher Hector has a motto, 'pass it on'. But
in a conversation, we do not simply passively 'pass
it on'. We investigate, question, respond, we use
our own creativity. And this is what we should do
with the canon: we should ask why, how, who; we
should interrogate it and explore beyond it.

All that I've written above stems from the

metaphor of 'literature is a living conversation'. Like a conversation, it's to do with communication and can be about anything. As in a conversation, in which both what we say and how we say it are important, literature shapes experience and provides meaning through form. The creativity of literature, just as in conversations, comes not from one side but in the dialogue, and it draws all aspects of ourselves into it. Our reactions to works of literature change as we age. Like a conversation, literature is not timeless but time-full: a past, visible in various ways, including the historical context of a work and the 'family trees' of influence and genre; a present (it's always read now); and a future (that would be you, joining the conversation). Like a proper dialogue, which points to a kind of equality between people, literature has a link to personal and political freedom. And like a dialogue, this can be easily corrupted by others, or by our own selves, as we exclude, refuse to listen or ban people from talking.

I said that metaphors are the tools of thought, and like all tools, metaphors are useful: a hammer helps us build; a camera preserves an image. But tools can also be dangerous or misleading: not only does a carelessly handled hammer hurt, but, more significantly, a person with a hammer can think that everything looks like a nail; a photo on your phone looks like – but isn't – the whole picture. So it's also true that the metaphor 'literature is a living conversation' covers up the fact that books don't really come alive, they can't answer questions you ask them: reading is only *like* speaking. A hand does not really come out from a text to take yours. Indeed, this metaphor passes over one of the most powerful technologies we possess as species: writing, the ability to preserve words and meanings across time and space. This ancient technology underlies many of our contemporary technologies (and their abuses: 'fake news' is not new to literature). Writing means that the 'living' part of the metaphor is less convincing because although writing is still a form of conversation (think of texts, posts or updates), it is not alive. But oddly, the fact that a work is in writing draws attention to the idea that the creativity of literature isn't just in the head of the famous author but also in us. When you read a text, it's not the author talking to you, as if she or he appeared in a puff of smoke, but the text talking *with* you and your creative response.

This chapter has used a metaphor, 'literature is a living conversation', to try to think about the ways in which literature works and has meaning. Rather than offer a map, it has tried to be the walk itself. To be honest, I don't worry too much about not being able to define literature. Some people find the lack of definition frustrating and this means they can feel a bit lost ('Excuse me. Can you tell me where I am?'); but I think that exactly this quality of being indefinable makes literature exciting, important and is part of why it can help you find who you are ('In our country, this is the way we say hello'). Literature is what makes matters matter. We become ourselves through literature; through stories, poems; through the creative and responsive uses of language. Thinking of literature through the metaphor of dialogue and conversation helps us grasp how this happens and its significance. Indeed, literature is a crucial part of our constant dialogue about humanity's ever-changing self-understanding – not about what we are but about who we are.

2

Studying Literature

The point of this book is not only to explain why literature matters but also to explain why the *study* of literature matters. Following the 'literature is a living conversation' metaphor from the previous chapter, it's already clear that literature and its study are similar in some profound way: an activity made by a kind of dialogue, and not simply a passive description of books you've read. At the deepest level, for example, both literature and its study draw on the same creativity. This is why the first of Stephen King's rules for writing is that if 'you want to be a writer, you must do two things above all others: read a lot and write a lot'.[1] He means not only that to be good at anything you have to pay attention to how it's done, but also that, at root, both reading and writing are the same dialogue. But even though all reading is creative, not everyone wants to be a writer, so why should we study literature? What is the school and university subject of English or literary studies – and the many other closely related disciplines (modern languages, for example) – beyond just reading?

I want to explain what the study of literature is like through an analogy with sport (another figure of speech!).[2] People take exercise all the time: walking to work; sprinting for the bus. Sometimes this is a bit more formal: kicking a ball about in the park with friends; going running every Saturday morning; swimming regularly. And sometimes this is even more organized – leagues, competitions – all the way to taking part in a World Cup or Olympic Games. Running for the bus, a 5k around your local park and the 10,000 m in the Olympics are the same activity, but each on an increasingly formal and intense scale.

Similarly, the study of literature is an 'intensified version' of what we do every day with the language we use, the stories we tell and hear.[3] Everyone undertakes activities and games; formal sports are just the more intensified version. Everyone talks, tells stories, uses and responds to language; most read, watch films or TV: the study of these is the more formal version of our everyday responses.[4] You don't have to be a member of the national squad to enjoy playing a game with friends, or have a medal to show you have fun running in the park, but the intensification of exercise brings all sorts of new challenges and demands, as does the intensification of reading in literary studies. Like a sport, the study of literature is supposed to be fun, but not necessarily easy. Literary studies is a *skill or craft*: to get good at it, you need to know your way around and to develop yourself. And like sport, it is also a shared and communal *activity*.

Where the study of literature differs from a sport – where the analogy fails, in fact – is in how you do it. A sport has agreed rules, and indeed other academic subjects have established (if contested) methodologies. In literary studies, there is no unanimity on the rules or methodology. In fact, the question of methodology is *the most contentious question* in literary studies.

The range of disagreement about methodology in literary studies is total. At one end of the scale, the Nobel laureate T. S. Eliot wrote in 1920 that in criticism 'there is no method except to be very intelligent'.[5] Right at the other end, from the 1960s to the present, a series of critical movements have tried to turn the study of literature into a science, following a strict methodology. Like a science, in the 1960s and 1970s, these movements aimed to uncover invariable rules behind the working of stories or how words mean; these days, they turn to computing power or neuroscience to analyse texts. Despite this divergence, all the way from 'no method' to 'all method/like a science/a computer program', there's something in all these views. Eliot means that you have to pick out and think about what strikes you most from a poem or a novel: there's no rule or algorithm to teach you to choose one aspect over another. And it's also true that you can study any narrative, from the Old English poem *Beowulf* to the cartoon *Rick and Morty*, in terms of its basic narrative elements (think how one could classify all the roles in a story: the protagonist, the antagonist, the helper, and so on); in under a second, a computer can search all the novels from the nineteenth century to discover parallels; and Jodie Archer and Matthew L. Jockers demonstrate using databases that almost all best-sellers share 'symmetry in a plotline and a clear three-act structure'.[6]

However, I am going to suggest that, even if there is no shared method, there is a fundamental idea which motivates the study of literature, an idea which grows from literature itself and from the concept that its study is an intensification of our everyday use of language. Just as literature is like a 'living conversation', so too conversation underlies all literary studies. Literary studies is based in the experience and meaning of dialogue. This idea is not accepted by everyone (recall: methodology is the most contentious question!), but I make no excuse for explaining and arguing for it here. It has significant consequences for the study of literature.

Literary Studies as Dialogue and Dissensus

Two of the most famous, insightful and passionate British literary critics of the twentieth century were husband and wife F. R. Leavis (1895–1978) and Q. D. Leavis (1906–81), and they put this idea of dialogue at the core of how they understood the study of literature. Their ideal form of critical debate was begun by a suggestion about a text: 'This is so, isn't it?' and the response would be 'Yes, but. . . .' These discussions would have no final answer and would be based on no simple equation or assessment objective. Perhaps equally as important was the idea that they would have no motivating principle except what the Leavises called 'life'. Some have suggested that 'life' is a total mystification. What does 'life' mean? Is my idea of 'life' the same as yours or theirs? The generation of critics that came after the Leavises and responded to their work argued that their sense of 'life' was unquestioningly tied into their class, race, position and age, and there's something to this. But by contrast, everyone sort of knows what 'life' is, even if they can't strictly define it. Indeed, part of the point of 'life' is that my version and understanding and yours differ because it can't be defined. Real conversations about literature – and real learning together – begin because in or for *my* 'life' a novel means *that* and in or for *your* 'life' it means *this*. As is often the way with critics, the Leavises' tone, the strength and severity of their judgements, gave them the reputation of literary critical tyrants, which almost completely belied the dialogical ideal of their work.

This idea of collaboration and dialogue underlying the study of literature was not limited to the Leavises and the many critics they influenced. In the USA too, the sense developed that criticism was a joint venture. In his influential essay 'Criticism, Inc.' (1937), the American poet and critic John Crowe Ransom (1888–1974) argued for a 'precise and systematic' criticism which was 'developed by the collective and sustained effort of learned persons': a literary version of how expert professionals – lawyers, accountants – work together in incorporated companies (the 'Inc.' of the title).[7] While it's true that one aspect of literature is as a product (it's sold in bookshops, after all), I'm not convinced that the study of literature is best understood metaphorically as a business. Although it is good for your career, as I discuss in chapter 4, literary studies doesn't primarily create products or services, for example. However, Ransom's sense of collaboration – and, ideally, the active, thoughtful and trusting cooperation which characterizes the best corporations – gets at the sense of dialogue. Similarly, in Soviet Russia, the thinker and critic M. M. Bakhtin (1895–1975) through his study of language and fiction outlined the 'dialogical imagination'. For him, literature and everyday language are made up of many different voices in conversation with each other, and freedom is built and maintained through these contrasting and conflicting voices. His work suggests, necessarily obliquely because of the Stalinist totalitarian rule under which he suffered, that those who seek to dominate this conversation and arrest it completely – shouting, accusing, excluding – are tyrannous.[8]

One major consequence of this sense of dialogue is that literary studies aims to do something different from most disciplines. In science, and in forms of philosophy, the point is to develop and agree *con*sensus propositions about the world and then progress to the next problem; in literary studies the aim is to help develop a continuing *dis*sensus about

29

the texts we study in order to root, explore and develop our own selves and distinctiveness. This is why F. R. Leavis writes that collaboration 'may take the form of disagreement, and one is grateful to the critics whom one has found worth disagreeing with'.[9] (If this seems weird, recall that people play sport both with and against each other.) If literature helps us think about who we are in our individuality, its intensified study develops this in a more communal and challenging way. But this fundamental difference of literary studies from other subjects, through its basis in dialogue, has a wider implication.

Literary Studies as a Different Model of Education

The idea that English, or literary studies, is a cooperative dialogue means that the discipline offers a view of a wholly different idea of what education really could and should be. This is most clearly understood by looking at the important and inspirational work of the Brazilian educationalist and activist Paulo Freire (1921–97), which specifically explores the importance of dialogue. His key book *Pedagogy of the Oppressed* (1968) reforms and rethinks education by focusing on its structure: to put this in the terms of literary studies, he asks us to pay attention to the *form* of the teaching as much as the *content* of the lecture or lesson. Crucially (like the Leavises), he links the form of education to ethics and (unlike the Leavises) to power.

Freire argues that education often follows what he calls the 'banking' model: information is simply 'deposited' by the teacher in the student's head, just as today we talk of 'downloading' information. The banking (or downloading) model assumes that students are simply empty buckets (or memory chips) to be filled; their minds are empty and they have nothing to bring to the lesson; they have no choice in how or what they are taught; the teacher acts and the students are acted upon; and the teacher is the one with knowledge and authority which the students simply accept. If we think of a lesson as a sentence with a subject, object and verb, then 'the teacher (*subject*) teaches (*verb*) the students (*object*)'. In this banking model of education, the subject of the lesson is the teacher, the students are simply the objects: the teacher does the lesson to the students. Freire writes that this banking concept of education assumes that people are

31

adaptable, manageable beings. The more students work at storing the deposits entrusted to them, the less they develop the critical consciousness which would result from their intervention in the world as transformers of that world. The more completely they accept the passive role imposed on them, the more they tend simply to adapt to the world as it is and to the fragmented view of reality deposited in them.[10]

This form of teaching makes students into passive regurgitators of information rather than active participants in their own education. (Let's stop for a second to think how truly odd that is: the downloading or banking model means that students are not the most important people *in the process of their own education.*)

In contrast, Freire offers a very different model of education: as you can guess from what I've written, he insists that teaching must be a dialogue. In an authentic dialogue, a conversation rather than an occasion for being ordered about, shouted at, and so on, people are in some sense equal, so both the teacher and student are subjects. Crucially, this means that knowledge is not simply deposited or downloaded but developed in the process of teaching and learning. ('It is an act of creation,' Freire writes.[11]) Everything, not simply what is formally stamped as 'knowledge', is brought to the experience. More than this, it 'is in speaking their word that people, by naming the world, transform it', and 'dialogue imposes itself as the way by which they achieve significance as human beings'.[12] This may sound idealistic – as indeed it is – but Freire is trying to get to the core of all that he sees that education should be. He was keen that his ideas did not harden into a set method but were constantly reinvented for different contexts and subjects: taking up his thinking can be a challenge for students and teachers.[13]

Yet if we think of literature and its study as a dialogue, we can understand how closely it is aligned with the image at the centre of Freire's vision of a different form of education. In a discussion of literature, each person, teacher or student, brings themselves, their own ideas, creativity and understanding, to the discussion and, through dialogue, they invent new knowledge. An academic friend of mine joked that no one teaching literature had ever got beyond sitting down with a seminar group, taking out the poem or novel and saying: 'Well, what do we make of this then?' But this light-hearted comment is actually spot on. In teaching literature, 'we' (the whole group, not the teacher depositing information down to the students) 'make' something (that is, create new knowledge) from our encounter with a literary text. You can see that this is very different from other forms of education. Freire's idea of teaching as dialogue sounds very idealistic. How might it work in a whole system of education, or in a curriculum?

Literary Studies as 'Knowledge-in-Action'

This is the question at the core of the work of the American educationalist Arthur Applebee (1946–2015), and it informs the title of his most influential book, *Curriculum as Conversation* (1996). In it he analyses not only the face-to-face processes of learning and teaching as a dialogue, but also the whole curriculum as a conversation across time, and discusses 'knowledge-in-action'.

If you have studied English at school, your learning has been influenced, behind the scenes and unknown to you, by the work of American literary critic and educationalist E. D. Hirsch. Through rather a selective reading of some psychology experiments, Hirsch argued that 'background knowledge' plays a crucial role in understanding texts. (Basically, he meant that if you already knew about the American Civil War, reading a novel about the American Civil

War would be easier.) From this, he developed the very influential idea of 'cultural literacy': if you had downloaded lots of facts about culture, reading and interpretation would become more straightforward. As well as being influential in the USA, this idea underlies the reforms led by the former education secretary Michael Gove and others which have shaped English teaching in the UK.

Applebee identifies two main problems with Hirsch's idea. First, Hirsch's view of what culture was important 'showed little awareness of the accomplishments of women, of people of color, or of anyone outside the Western tradition'; remember, literature is like a living conversation for everyone.[14] But, as Applebee quite fairly writes, this could be remedied simply by broadening the list of what counted as culture.

The second problem is more significant, but also harder for those who are not teachers or students to understand (people like politicians and polemical journalists, for example). Applebee argues that Hirsch's idea may give students lists of background facts, but these 'catalogs of information frustrate rather than encourage conversational action'; so rather than helping students open up and be in dialogue with literary texts, 'cultural literacy' 'seems destined to shut them out'.[15] What he means is this:

if you are studying Charlotte Brontë's *Jane Eyre* (1847) and an authority figure bombards you with a catalogue of historical facts about the novel and its nineteenth-century context, this knowledge may drown out your own responses, ideas and interpretation and leave you feeling ignorant and, probably, a bit intimidated, as if what you know or have read means nothing. You may have to learn this catalogue of formal knowledge almost as if by rote and you may not be able to relate the items in it to your everyday life. (You use a catalogue – or an internet search engine – to search *for* something. By itself, a catalogue is just a meaningless collection of facts and items. It is your *interaction* with it, your search – for shoes, for games with robot dinosaurs in them, for a deeper understanding of *Jane Eyre* – which makes it meaningful.)

This common experience – learning as 'downloading a catalogue' – has three damaging effects if you are a student of literature. First, if you have been told that *Jane Eyre* is about the oppression of women in the Victorian period (it's how the catalogue has presented it, and it's not incorrect), then that's what you are expected to spot and talk about. In contrast, the moments in which the novel questions or subverts this idea or where it explores other aspects of the world falls out of focus or even becomes invisible because you are concentrating your gaze so intently on making the novel fit the data from the catalogue. (And recall: literature escapes definition, and so the catalogue is working to define precisely what can't be easily defined.) Ironically, many exam resources and even wonderful Wikipedia (which, after all, is an encyclopaedia, a catalogue of knowledge) exacerbate exactly this problem.

Second, the creation of an exclusive specialist knowledge which has to be downloaded or deposited means that everything else you might bring to understanding the book (TV boxsets you've watched, similar books, memes you've thought about, comics – really anything which isn't in the catalogue) is made to seem unimportant and irrelevant. Which, of course, it isn't: interpreting literature is about *everything* you know and all of you.

Third, and I think worst, *you* are made to seem irrelevant. *Jane Eyre* is the story of a girl growing up, going to school, being bullied, standing up for herself, making friends, growing to be a woman, finding work and then falling in love. These are life experiences, or situations, many of which we share, and when we read the book, we are in dialogue with them: these should be part of how you interpret, talk with, live with the novel and make it yours. If you are told *Jane Eyre* is just an example of a 'Victorian religious conversion narrative' with a twist, this is interesting, of course, but it isn't in conversation with you, and it's the novel's conversation with you that makes literature, and literary studies, matter.

Applebee is not dismissive of this idea of 'cultural literacy' (as some educators have been): of course, you need some factual knowledge and the *content* of the curriculum you are taught is important. But – to put this in literary studies terms again – focusing on the content too much means we don't pay attention to the form. Cultural literacy is educational fast food: easy to make and cheap to offer, not really nutritious and often regurgitated or excreted without digestion. Instead, Applebee wants to stress what he calls 'knowledge-in-action': how you bring yourself and all your formal and informal knowledge to your learning; how you respond to learning; and the idea that learning is a shared activity, not simply a series of facts to be downloaded and cut-and-pasted. And, working with the metaphor that literature is a living conversation, literary studies must be a shared, dialogical activity.

Literary Studies as Craft and Activity

We can see aspects of this dialogical nature and 'knowledge-in-action' by looking at two 'hands on' aspects of the study of literature: first, the craft often reductively called 'metaphor-spotting', and sometimes encouraged by schools, exams and assessment objectives; second, the activity often called close analysis, practical criticism, critical reading or 'unseens' – properly, this is called *close reading*. Neither of these is a methodology. The first is more like a *skill or craft* because you learn how to do it and you can improve at it, just as one does with any skill. The second is an activity because really it's a shared and communal action.

The Craft of 'Metaphor-Spotting'

Students in literary studies are often taught to 'metaphor-spot': to learn how to identify and pluck metaphors as if they were botanists in the countryside picking wild flowers for their collecting cases. It seems a bit clinical, maybe, to turn, say, wild garlic, hawthorn, honeysuckle, lavender, love-in-idleness, marjoram, marigold, primrose, lily of the valley, forget-me-not and sweet violet into quantifiable biological samples, though perhaps it's a necessary part of the process of becoming a botanist (and the word 'anthology', in which people collect literary texts, meant, originally, a collection of flowers). But for students of literary studies, this process leads to the very mistaken idea that poetry is a kind of basic message to which floral decoration is added, and that their job is simply to classify the flowers. This is – almost – completely the wrong way round and upside down.

Metaphors are everywhere: our everyday language is full of 'figures of speech' or (more formally) tropes. Trope is a term originally developed from the Greek word *tropos*, meaning 'turn', and it signifies a moment where language has turned away from its literal meaning. We use tropes all the time. (There, look! 'All the time' is not literally true. I really meant: we use them often. 'All the time' is the trope called 'hyperbole', which means 'an enormous exaggeration'.) Metaphors understand one thing as another: to say 'the heat of passion' is to take a concept from one set of ideas (temperature) and translate it to another (emotion). The metaphor that passion is hot is such a cliché that we hardly recognize it as a metaphor any more: it's a dead metaphor (just like 'all the time'). But poetic language works to *defamiliarize* language in striking ways. Here is the classical Greek poet Sappho:

> For whenever I look at you even briefly
> I can no longer say a single thing . . .
> instantly a delicate flame runs beneath my skin.[16]

The same metaphor (love = heat) but suddenly strange, beautiful and powerful: a delicate flame under the skin. In their book *Metaphors We Live By* (2003), George Lakoff and Mark Johnson argue that both living literary and everyday dead metaphors rely on what they call very widely understood (if rarely noticed) basic conceptual metaphors.[17] Both 'the heat of passion' and 'a delicate flame runs beneath my skin' rely on the idea that love is hot. These basic conceptual metaphors are everywhere: in all our language, media, rhetoric, literature. Indeed, these 'conceptual metaphors' structure our thought itself.

Spotting these metaphors is a craft, certainly. For example, an analogue clock is a visual metaphor: it measures the passage of time by using the space from one hour to the next on its face as a metaphor for time. Once you see this, then the basic conceptual metaphor of 'time as space' suddenly appears everywhere. To describe life as a journey is to describe 'time as space'.

But this craft of 'metaphor-spotting' becomes more important when the significance of metaphors

41

becomes clearer. The contemporary philosopher of science Daniel Dennett writes that 'metaphors are not just metaphors; metaphors are the tools of thought ... so it is important to equip yourself with the best set of tools available'.[18] We use metaphors to express our thinking. Sappho again: 'You set me on fire.'[19] But we also use them to expand our thought: hot love can go cold; a fire needs feeding. More significantly, we also use metaphors to think creatively: if my love is like fire, then is it warm and reassuring (like a log fire on a cold night) or wild (like an uncontrollable forest blaze)? And we use them to judge: fire is beneficial, but also dangerous. Might I burn myself? Might I hurt another? Metaphors also smuggle in ideas (just as 'literature is a living conversation' did in the previous chapter) which grab us without us noticing: the French philosopher Jacques Derrida warned of their 'metaferocity'. Fires, measured or wild and unrestrained, don't last; fire consumes everything; but we need fire to live.

What this means for the study of English is that when you are taught the craft of metaphor-spotting, you are not really being taught to single some flower out from the hedgerow. Rather, by picking that flower, you are having your attention drawn to the whole ecosystem surrounding us, of which, say, the primrose is but one tiny example. One metaphor opens up to all of our language, literary and everyday, in your life and the life of everyone you know. More, you are taking up the tools to shape and form your world. People's thinking is shaped by these basic conceptual metaphors: learning to understand them and use them not only helps us to understand ourselves but also helps us understand and talk with others.

The Activity of Close Reading

If understanding metaphor is a craft, then close reading – looking at a text in intense detail – is one of the most important activities of literary studies: not a methodology; rather a 'persistent feature', or practice.[20] Almost every single student of literary studies learns how to close read, but sometimes, ironically, without learning that this kind of reading *is* a practice and an activity. (This is a bit like kicking a football without knowing there is a sport called football!) It often seems as if it's the natural way to do English. And in a way, that's right: like everything in literary studies, close reading is just an 'intensified version' of what we might normally do when we pay special attention to a piece of text. (Think of how you might pore over a message, a tweet, a status update from someone you like.) But like every practice we undertake, close reading has a history and an origin story.

In the early days of the discipline of English, a student at the University of Cambridge, William Empson, and his lecturer, I. A. Richards, were discussing Shakespeare's Sonnet 129, which begins: 'Th' expense of spirit in a waste of shame/Is lust in action.' Richards describes how Empson, taking the sonnet 'as a conjuror takes his hat . . . produced an endless swarm of lively rabbits from it' as he pulled out different interpretations of the poem. He ended by saying, 'You could do that with any poetry, couldn't you?' Richards, a bit overwhelmed, replied that, 'You'd better go off and do it, hadn't you?' What Empson wrote for his tutor was the core of his celebrated book *Seven Types of Ambiguity* (1930). Despite the authoritative-sounding title, and as many readers have discovered, the types of ambiguity are quite, well, ambiguous and often not as clearly distinct as one would like. Even Richards wrote that reading too much of the book in one go was like having flu, but 'read a little with care and your reading habits may be altered – for the better'.[21] The point of the book is not the classification of types but the idea of *ambiguity*, 'any verbal nuance, however slight, which gives room for alternative reactions to the same piece of language'.[22]

Close reading is alive to ambiguity, shifts in meaning, doubling, hints and associations. It is less interested in the historical context or the author's biography (you don't even need to know who the author is to do a close reading of their work) and more interested in the 'words on the page'. Indeed, this phrase became a slogan for a quite extraordinarily influential group of writers and academics in the USA who enthusiastically adopted close reading and became known as the New Critics. In contrast to the historicist critics I mentioned in the first chapter, they are often described as 'formalist' critics.

Significantly for literary studies, the aim of close reading is unlike that of other kinds of reading: lawyers, scientists and historians, for example, try to cut down ambiguity, to avoid doubt. But in close reading the point is to respond to the 'simultaneous presence of many meanings' rather than draw out one unambiguously.[23] Reading a literary text is unlike code-breaking (to which it is sometimes incorrectly compared) because it doesn't aim at uncovering one particular (secret) message. Instead, close reading is attuned to multiple meanings and associations which open up a literary text in and for conversation. This interest in 'opening up' is one characteristic which makes literary studies a different subject from all others. Close reading is an open-ended, hard-to-pin-down and shared creative activity.

The origin of close reading isn't, really, quite as simple as this rabbit-from-a-hat 'eureka moment' suggests. The ideas behind close reading had been brewing for some time before Empson's conjuror's trick. Richards himself, for example, had been getting students to read 'unseen passages' with no details of the author or context. And a generation earlier, Richard Moulton, a teacher in adult education, had developed a similar way of reading literature.[24] But this 'origin story' does reveal something of what close reading is as a practice. Moreover, it is a practice that became very widespread because, done properly, close reading is a superb and dialogical way of teaching and learning, and does not need huge libraries, specialist knowledge – or even access to Wikipedia. (I'll discuss it in more detail in chapter 4.)

Like any skill, you get better at close reading the more you do it. You learn to find your way around literary texts and intensify their use of language; you begin to recognize the shifting forms of association and meaning and, as with skilfulness in any area of life, you become more confident in your own reading, in bringing yourself to a text. You 'make a reading', you develop a sense of what a text means.

And there is an inventive pleasure in the shaping of a meaning (like pulling rabbits out of a hat). Indeed, close reading is like the creative counterpoint to, or reverse engineering of, the writer's craft which understands that writing is not simply about the content of a communication, but about its form as well: a *what* and a *how* together. Close reading involves thinking like a poet; or, rather, as this chapter began, both writing and reading literature involve taking part in a creative conversation.

But – and this is a point almost always missed in discussions of this topic, and yet one that is extraordinarily important for literary studies and why it matters – close reading is not just a skill but an *activity*, something you *do* with others, as an open-ended conversation with the literary text. Because it is done with others, it is different from the use of skill, which can be done alone: in an action, not only do you not know quite what is going to happen in the end (or even where the end is), but also the significance (and joy, perhaps) is in the *shared doing*. There is a shared, if fleeting, creative delight in the communal shaping of meaning, of agreement and of disagreement, of distinctiveness and of similarity.

Thinking of close reading as an activity has positive consequences. Book groups around the world discover over and over again the joy of reading and talking together. More, close reading focuses attention not only on what is obviously in the text, but on other, often sub-textual meanings: it uncovers a deeper view of 'what's going on' which surprisingly often goes against what you expect. This works with both fiction and non-fiction (there's an example in the next chapter). Close reading has been contentious (everything in literary studies is open to argument) because in its focus on the 'words on the page' it seems to cut the literary text out of history, out of its context. Yet Terry Eagleton, a critic much concerned with history and context, finds in the practice of close reading precisely the opposite:

> Language is the medium in which both Culture and culture – literary art and human society – come to consciousness, and literary criticism is thus a sensitivity to the thickness and intricacy which makes us what we are. Simply by attending to its own distinctive object, it can have fundamental implications for the destiny of culture as a whole.[25]

That is, becoming attuned to the words of a literary text also makes us attentive to the world, and the language of the world, in which we live.

But thinking of close reading as an activity also has some negative consequences. An especially irritating one for someone like me is that whatever I write about close reading does not get close to the activity of actually doing it.

I could describe how I and a group of readers developed our thoughts about a text and show how our ideas changed as we listened to each other; I could give you examples of wonderful moments of acute readings; I could film a group talking. But these are only the results of a close reading, the residue of the chemical reaction itself, and might easily end up like the 'downloading' of historical context I criticized above. These kinds of descriptions of the activity are not 'the next best thing': they are a completely different thing to the experience of it, as writing about sex is different from the experience of sex. However, in the next chapter, I'm going to show, in a detailed example, the results of such a close reading.

It has another frustrating consequence for academics in English trying to explain why their discipline matters. Historians aim to create narratives about the past, which easily become lectures, podcasts or TV programmes. Scientists often make things, or reveal things about the world; it's easy to see why these matter when you stop to think about the technological marvel of the smartphone in your hand. But if the core event of your discipline happens in a dialogical activity with a small group of involved people, you can't do this on TV, YouTube or a podcast. Doing an activity together is not the same as doing it alone or telling someone about it: you might be skilled at kicking a ball accurately, or describing a game to a friend, but neither of these are the same *as playing sport together*. (The same is true for sex too, of course.) Finally, this aspect of close reading as an activity always means it's a risk: any shared activity can fail. No one might come to the party; the political demonstration might be a squib; we've all sat through – or taught – boring lessons that have failed. In close reading a text, everyone in the group is responsible for the activity being rewarding, interesting, enjoyable. As an activity, it needs a team. The activity of close reading is more than a catalogue of facts. Like being good at sport, it can't easily be written down or described. Nearly a century old, and surviving ups and downs of literary critical fashion, this core practice still goes on, passed down through the activity of learning and teaching of literature.

Conclusion

In this chapter I've argued that, just as literature can be understood metaphorically as a living conversation, so literary studies can be seen in the same way: underneath all the different ideas about how we should study literature is the idea of dialogue. Dialogue helps us discover our own distinctiveness as people and underlies the best ideas about what education itself should be: a creative act which transforms ourselves, others and the world. In Applebee's idea of 'knowledge-in-action' we find a way of studying literature that reflects this, as well as getting a sense of pitfalls to avoid. I focused on two linked common examples of things done in literary studies, in English seminars and lessons, thinking about metaphors and the activity of close reading.

This sense that literary studies is a dialogue teaches us what the subject should not be. It should not exclude people from the conversation: just as in everyday life, this is hurtful and wrong and it also misses out on the chance to hear other insights or fascinating ideas. Literary studies is not or shouldn't be made of lists or catalogues: a list of ten top books might be attention-grabbing but this is not an education in literature. A more sophisticated version of this 'catalogue thinking' is an overemphasis on the historical context of a poem, play or novel. As I suggested above, downloading this catalogue with the implication that it provides the only answer can mean that understanding the text on your own terms is harder and make your own reactions seem ignorant and irrelevant. Yet your thoughts and feelings are the most significant first response to a work of literature. When the subject loses its dialogical form, it's not doing what it should.

English and literary studies should – and, at their best, do – offer a sense of the dialogue that education really is, rather than the downloading, depositing or assessment-objective tick-boxing it can become. An English lesson creates knowledge in the activity and discussion of literature, and takes on board not just 'what you know about the text', what you have learned formally, but also what you've picked up from your life: what you feel and all you are. Knowledge about literature overflows the more constrained categories of knowledge in other subjects because *you* are central to your reading of literature. This is why the study of literature is revealing; this is why it can change us; this is why some people don't like it or find it dangerous or risky, and why others embrace it. It should be an exciting and perhaps disconcerting process: literary studies should challenge you not only in what you read but also through the ideas of the others reading with you.[26]

3

Why Does Literature Matter?

Literature and works of literature matter in so many different ways that there is no single, easy-to-point-to answer to this question: just as literature can't be defined, so how it matters can't be pinned down. Here, I'm going to choose one concrete example of how and why literature matters, using the work of psychologists and literary critics and drawing on ideas of dialogue, close reading and the analysis of metaphors from the previous chapter. But I've chosen this particular approach specifically so that, in the second half of the chapter, I can use another concrete example to address the widely held idea that literature doesn't or shouldn't matter at all.

Why Does Literature Matter?

The Reader Project

Jane Davis, an academic at the University of Liverpool, sought *something else* from her study of literature. Teaching showed her that literature offered 'a kind of meaning and connection' not found elsewhere, 'something real to carry home when day is done', as the American author Saul Bellow writes.[1] But this was not enough.

> Things crystallised one day when I was driving to the university to teach Wordsworth's 'Ode: Intimations of Immortality'.[2] It was spring and there were daffodils lining the path to the door of an ex-council house opposite the traffic lights where I had stopped in North Birkenhead. The daffodils were dancing, and the door was opened by a younger woman in her pyjamas with a baby, perhaps a year old, on her arm. He seemed to leap up with joy at the sight of the older woman and I thought, 'the babe leaps up on his mother's arm', a line from the 'Immortality Ode' I had been reading earlier that day. At exactly the same moment that the line came into my mind, a thought also exploded: that child will never read Wordsworth. He'll never think 'the babe leaps up' or know 'The Daffodils'. He can't have this stuff which has made a life for me. He will get a bad education, not including any of the joy and usefulness of poetry.[3]

Why Does Literature Matter?

She set up a summer outreach project called 'Get into reading'. A small group read out loud a poem, 'Crossing the Bar', by Tennyson.[4] One of the women in the group began to cry. 'In twenty-odd years at the university, I had never seen anyone moved to tears by a poem, but here we were, in a room in a community centre in Birkenhead, and a woman was crying.' Davis goes on:

In two other such groups, people cried when I read this poem. Why? My dad died last year and it reminds me of him, said one woman. My daughter died six weeks ago, said another. It reminds me of my father, he died when I was fourteen, another told me. That line about the tide, 'but such a tide as moving seems asleep' reminds me of when we would walk together and the Mersey would be high and full ... Of course, I knew that literature was personal, and had experienced that myself, both close-up in private, and at some distance in my university teaching, but now without the screen of 'teaching', without 'university course', without 'classroom', the stuff of feeling was exposed as live ammunition: powerful emotional things could and would happen because of the words coming to life in our minds. After the woman whose daughter had died got through the session, crying all the while, a man, an ex-welder, leaned across the table and took her hand. 'Well done, kidder,' he said. I knew at that point that I had stumbled into something extraordinary. . . . This was the *something else*.[5]

Davis went on to found the Reader project, which works to build on precisely this: 'By bringing people together to read great literature aloud we are improving well-being, reducing social isolation and building stronger communities across the UK and beyond.'[6] Perhaps, to use the ideas from the previous chapter, you might say that Davis had found a way to avoid the 'banking model' of education – the 'screen of "teaching" . . . "university course" . . . "classroom"', the demand to download a catalogue into her students' heads – and brought to the surface the underlying concept of dialogue which is the foundation of any real engagement with literature.

One scheme that the Reader project ran was with mental health groups in South London, doing the 'shared reading' described above. Small groups of service users would gather, read a poem together and talk about it. The responses, compiled in a report called *What Literature Can Do*, were striking. One group member, Peter, said:

> And you suddenly think, God! I have got an imagination. I can sense that. I have got something to say. It makes you feel like a fully-functioning person

again. You know, like a member of society. Whereas your world was very small often, on your own and lonely, or with other drug users when you'd be in your comfort zone. You suddenly felt like a living, breathing important, credible person because you could understand good literature, you could see the colour, you could relate to the people, you could relate it to yourself and the world you're in.[7]

Another, Arthur, stressed how in reading literature 'you do the feelings – imagine, express, read aloud, perform, and feel them as acts'.[8] Others found also that poetry gave them a way to encounter their own intangible realities: Jackie said that poetry showed her that there was more than simply appeared on the surface and 'it's what we can't see that is life'.[9] Older group members suffering dementia found poems accessed emotional memories and reoriented their lifestories. Many readers learned about themselves and others from the shifting perspectives that literary texts offer. Very many experienced a deep change: '"I never quite knew I thought or felt that" or "I never knew I could admit that thought or use that feeling": "one thing you have given me is a voice".'[10] As with close reading, which I discussed in the previous chapter, shared reading is not just a talking but a doing, a communal activity. The report concluded that 'what literature can do above all is

(1) trigger access to felt experience at the human core and (2) offer a freer, deeper and more mobile way of thinking about it'.[11]

This is one way to express how literature matters and, with the Reader project, act on it. But this idea of literature is treated with contempt by many, especially those in public and political life. Instead they say . . .

'Now, what I want is, Facts.'

Mr Gradgrind is one of Charles Dickens' most memorable villains. A factory owner, he dominates the fictional Coketown, where *Hard Times* (1854) is set; he's a Dickensian Montgomery Burns from *The Simpsons* (or, actually, Burns is a *Simpsons* Gradgrind). He has an interest in education and has set up a school. But what does the school teach?

Here he is at the very start of the novel, instructing one of the teachers in front of the students:

Now, what I want is, Facts. Teach these boys and girls nothing but Facts. Facts alone are wanted in life. Plant nothing else, and root out everything else. You can only form the minds of reasoning animals upon Facts: nothing else will ever be of any service to them. This is the principle on which I bring up

my own children, and this is the principle on which
I bring up these children. Stick to the Facts, sir![12]

Gradgrind has no time for fiction, for poetry, for
the felt experience of the human core. Indeed, his
name has entered the language as '*one who is hard
and cold, and solely interested in facts*'. This is, of
course, the opposite of the educational philosophy
of the Leavises, who saw Gradgrind as a monster.
And it's also the opposite of Paulo Freire's view of
the right way to educate people: when Freire writes
that the 'banking' or 'downloading' model of education turns the students 'into "containers", into
"receptacles" to be filled by the teacher',[13] he clearly
had *this* chapter of *this* novel in mind. Gradgrind
sees the students as 'little vessels then and there
arranged in order, ready, to have imperial gallons
of facts poured into them until they were full to the
brim'.[14] The 'gallons of facts' are means for him
to make the students useful as tools in his factory;
useful in his you-scratch-my-back-I-scratch-yours
view of life, for it

was a fundamental principle of the Gradgrind
philosophy that everything had to be paid for.
Nobody was ever on any account to give anybody
anything, or render anybody help without purchase.
Gratitude was to be abolished . . . every inch of the

existence of mankind, from birth to death, was to
be a bargain across a counter.[15]

Everything – every inch of life - is reduced for
Gradgrind to money, to a financial exchange.

Gradgrind is – at least at the start – a satirical
character: the novel is attacking the philosopher
and reformer Jeremy Bentham (1748–1832) and
the philosophy he invented, utilitarianism. The core
idea of this philosophy is that 'it is the greatest
happiness of the greatest number that is the meas-
ure of right and wrong', where happiness means
more experience of pleasure than of pain. To this
end, Bentham invented what he called the 'hedonic
calculus', which was a way of working out what to
do: how much and what sort of pleasure will any
act create? Utilitarianism is an instrumental philosophy: everything is simply an instrument, a tool
to create pleasure or pain. For Bentham, this means
that literature – all art and culture in fact – is simply
one tool amongst others. He wrote that, putting our
conventional ideas of the greatness of literature and
art to one side, 'the game of push-pin is of equal
value with the arts and sciences of music and poetry.
If the game of push-pin furnished more pleasure, it
is more valuable than either.'[16] In Bentham's world-
view, therefore, great books and push-pin – today's

version would be Candy Crush or another of those simple-but-so-addictive game apps on your phone – are equivalent in that they simply absorb people's attention and make 'pleasure'.

One of Bentham's friends and disciples was James Mill (1773–1836), who decided to bring his son up following utilitarian ideas. So John Stuart Mill (1806–73) – who went on to become probably the most famous British thinker of the nineteenth century – studied Bentham from an early age and believed in his philosophy. But in his *Autobiography*, he writes of how 'I awakened from this as from a dream.'[17]

> It was in the autumn of 1826. I was in a dull state of nerves, such as everybody is occasionally liable to; unsusceptible to enjoyment or pleasurable excitement; one of those moods when what is pleasure at other times, becomes insipid or indifferent.

We'd call this depression, perhaps. Mill asks himself:

> 'Suppose that all your objects in life were realized; that all the changes in institutions and opinions which you are looking forward to, could be completely effected at this very instant: would this be a great joy and happiness to you?' And an irrepressible self-consciousness distinctly answered, 'No!' At this my heart sank within me: the whole foundation

> on which my life was constructed fell down. All my happiness was to have been found in the continual pursuit of this end. The end had ceased to charm, and how could there ever again be any interest in the means? I seemed to have nothing left to live for.

This despair didn't leave him: carrying on his normal active life, meeting with people, getting rest didn't help. And he felt that neither his friends, nor his father, whose upbringing had led him to this depression, could offer him the support needed. His favourite books – non-fiction, biographies, 'memorials of past nobleness and greatness from which I had always hitherto drawn strength and animation', left him low. 'I became persuaded, that my love of mankind, and of excellence for its own sake, had worn itself out.'

Mill writes that it was in the 'dry, heavy dejection of the melancholy winter of 1826–7' that 'a small ray of light broke in upon my gloom'. He read, by chance, an account of the death of the father of the French writer Jean-François Marmontel; an English translation was published in 1827. You can read the account online yourself;[18] it's very short and doesn't seem especially powerful, yet it moved Mill to tears.

> From this moment my burden grew lighter. The oppression of the thought that all feeling was dead

within me was gone. I was no longer hopeless: I was not a stock or a stone. I had still, it seemed, some of the material out of which all worth of character, and all capacity for happiness, are made. . . . Thus the cloud gradually drew off, and I again enjoyed life; and though I had several relapses, some of which lasted many months, I never again was as miserable as I had been.

This experience of depression and recovery led to two profound changes for Mill. First, he rejected utilitarianism. Happiness was not the right aim of life, but rather, he realized, it arises almost as a side-effect when a person focuses on something else: 'on the happiness of others, on the improvement of mankind, even on some art or pursuit, followed not as a means, but as itself an ideal end. Aiming thus at something else, they find happiness by the way.' In addition, happiness seems to escape analysis: 'Ask yourself whether you are happy, and you cease to be so.'

Second, and especially significant in a book about why literature matters, Mill came to understand that literature, art and culture were not like push-pin. Instead he realized that the 'internal culture of the individual' needs to be 'nourished and enriched'; not just by facts but also by feelings. And this led Mill to think again about the importance of poetry, and especially, for him, Wordsworth. What appealed to him wasn't Wordsworth's famous accounts of nature. (Mill said that the novelist Sir Walter Scott described nature better and even 'a very second-rate' landscape painting does that 'more effectually than any poet'.) Rather, says Mill, what grasped him was the expression of 'states of feeling, and of thought coloured by feeling' influenced by beauty, feelings that 'could be shared in by all human beings'. On reading, for example, the poem called the 'Immortality Ode', or 'Intimations of Immortality', Mill finds that Wordsworth had 'a similar experience to mine; that he also had felt that the first freshness of youthful enjoyment of life was not lasting; but that he had sought for compensation, and found it, in the way in which he was now teaching me to find it'. Not literature in general, but this specific poet had told him something about feeling and about life that spoke to him profoundly. Coming to be attuned to Wordsworth was a process for Mill, a kind of education: 'I seemed to learn what would be the perennial sources of happiness, when all the greater evils of life shall have been removed. And I felt myself at once better and happier as I came under their influence.'

These two insights by Mill – his new sense of how real happiness arises and his realization of the importance of art – encouraged him in his work as a reformer, a champion of the rights of women and a philosopher. This is one of the most moving and revealing accounts of why literature matters, and what Mill writes chimes with what many of the shared readers in the Reader project say.

The Professor of Happiness

But Mr Gradgrind has not left us. Indeed, he has a new career. A contemporary version of Bentham's assertion that push-pin (or Candy Crush) 'is of equal value with the arts and sciences of music and poetry' is made by the psychologist Paul Dolan, who works on the science of happiness. (His best friend, Mig, calls him the 'Professor of Happiness'.) Like Bentham, whom he tries to update, Dolan's basic idea is that happiness can be defined and measured: it is made up of doing things that are pleasurable (eating, watching TV, having sex) and that are purposeful (earning money, raising children, helping charities). To be happy 'you need to feel both pleasure and purpose', and this 'pleasure–purpose principle' is his version of Bentham's 'hedonic calculus'.[19] Underlying this principle and central to his book *Happiness by Design* is the conceptual metaphor that time is money. Dolan writes that each day 'you have a bank account with 1,440 minutes in it. Each day that bank account goes back to zero again, with no borrowing or saving.'[20] Our time – like our money – is scarce, and it's running out. Attention is how we spend our time, writes Dolan: we 'pay attention'.[21] His conclusion? 'Happiness is determined by how you allocate your attention' and unhappiness comes from 'misallocating your attention'.[22]

In literary studies, critics make a distinction between the real author – the person actually living and breathing – and the 'implied author', the way that the narrator or apparent author presents themselves in the text. We learn a lot about the implied Paul Dolan from *Happiness by Design*. He's happy; he mentions his wife and kids often; he was the first person in his family to go to university and so says he has a sense of the 'complexities and quirks of the real lives of people from a range of backgrounds'.[23] Like Bentham, the implied Dolan is a reformer, keen that we don't believe in silly stories. He likes jokes ('Humour helps social integration'[24]) and knows people care for one another ('I have conducted numerous studies that show we care greatly about the health of other people'[25]). Fundamentally, and like Gradgrind, he thinks we care for others because 'scratching someone else's back if they would scratch yours ... is good for your survival'.[26] From a newspaper interview we learn that he hates holidays and weddings, but likes imparting his 'pearls of wisdom to the next generation of opinion leaders or losers'.[27] He declares that 'I am generous with my money as well as my time' and that he has a 'ridiculously expensive – and unnecessarily big – Bang & Olufsen TV'; he loves 'going out ... and I'm bloody good at it too. Just ask my best mate, Mig, who lives in Ibiza.'

And he hates literature. He just can't see the point of it, and isn't shy at all about repeating this whenever he can.

> If I was an island, I would be Ibiza, to paraphrase Will in *About a Boy*. And just to be clear, I got this from the [2002] film and not the [1998 Nick Hornby] book: I have never read a novel in my life. There are only so many hours in the day and I have decided to fill them with activities other than reading made-up stories. Each to their own, eh?

Again, *Happiness by Design* is a 'chance to get something off my chest' about literature:

> [O]ver the years, many people have told me that I should read novels. I have never read a novel in my life (unless you count *Of Mice and Men* at

school – we were supposed to read *The Mayor of Casterbridge* but have you seen how long that is?)[28]

He asks: what if he read novels and they didn't make him any happier? For the implied Dolan, everything is only important for its 'instrumental value', for how it produces more happiness. Literature is just something else along with apps, the gym, push-pin, and so on. But his instrumentalism extends beyond novels:

> When people ask me how they can get happier, have more sex, lose weight and so on I reply that they should get happy friends and ditch the miserable ones, get friends who have lots of sex and ditch those who don't, get thin friends and ditch the overweight ones. Although I say this half-jokingly, you do need to think carefully about this.[29]

Think carefully (it's only half a joke): implied Dolan suggests that your friends are only tools to make you feel good. And (half a joke) if that's the role of your friends, what about your partner and your kids? (There's a weird dry, heavy, dejected moment when Dolan writes that 'it feels as if I sometimes give up both pleasure and purpose for my kids' happiness' and his wife 'definitely does'.[30] Bleak, if we recall his pleasure–purpose principle: half a joke, think carefully.)

I've spent some time discussing the implied figure of Paul Dolan because – as the story from Mill shows – your engagement with literature is somehow tied to the kind of person you are. Like Gradgrind, for the implied Dolan everything is a tool for use. And one step beyond, actually: for the implied Dolan, even fun, friendship and people (half a joke, think carefully) are just tools, too. If something is useful, it's valuable; if it's useless, it's worthless or silly. I quite admire his ability to call bullshit on what he thinks is bullshit.

Indeed, it might be easy simply to dismiss the implied Dolan, who is offering one contemporary example of this instrumentalist view. Of course the implied Dolan doesn't like literature because he believes that we are just things, that people are tools.

In contrast to this idea, I could just insist that people are not things and that literature matters because it is the indefinable expression of our 'not-thinginess': it's where instrumentalism is resisted. But I don't want to dismiss the implied Dolan: I want to take him totally seriously and engage with his work in a literary dialogue. The implied Dolan may hate weddings and holidays but he's also clearly happy, hard-working, successful, thoughtful, intelligent, reforming, humorous and fun. Why doesn't literature matter to him? I want to show it does *but he just doesn't acknowledge it*. And we can see that literature matters, oddly, from his own book. What he thinks is useless (just silly made-up stories) actually turns out to be the most useful aspect of *Happiness by Design*. Literature is the design of *Happiness by Design*.

Slowing down a bit and reading his book closely, spending some of our attention on it, it's clear that he actually *uses* literature and literary techniques all the time, just as, in his newspaper profile, he uses a metaphor – 'If I was an island, I would be Ibiza' – taken via a film from a novel. For example, the implied Dolan begins *Happiness by Design* getting us onside by telling us a secret 'confession' about how he overcame adversity. A story of how he resolved his stammer immediately makes us sympathetic to him: we can all identify with overcoming an obstacle. Again, the book itself has a narrative drive – the story of the pleasure–purpose principle' takes us, he writes, on a 'journey'.[31] And, as I've suggested, he has given a literary account of himself, his hopes, ambitions, doubts and fears. Further, the book is full of smaller stories: he explains how his friend Dixie trains for body-building competitions, and this narrative (warming up, developing, delivering) shapes the structure of the whole book. Just like the writers

I mentioned in chapter 1, he has reflectively told you how he wants his book to be read, following the metaphor of a body-building competition. The book also includes a couple of literary stories: he quotes at length a parable about a fisherman from Paul Coelho and also cites *Macbeth*. Dolan places useful metaphors throughout (as in a factory, there is a 'production process' in which you take 'income, health, etc., and convert them into happiness'[32]) and less useful ones (the picture of the pendulum, which sets pleasure against purpose, which is not really what he means). There's a literary mnemonic, an acrostic poem, really, in homage to a similar one composed by Bentham. Dolan focuses on words and their meanings (he pays attention to the phrase 'pay attention'). There are occasional jokes: the brain of our ancestor *Ardipithecus ramidus* is 'Ard-wired'[33] into us. And there are even some poetic moments, both energetic – his description of himself in the gym with the blood pumping in his ears – and melancholy ('Lost happiness is lost forever'[34]). Close reading shows that – quite against his view that literature is useless – it has been deeply and profoundly *useful to him*.

More, Dolan's work is successful because of its deep but unacknowledged (by him) literary characteristics. In the previous chapter I discussed basic conceptual metaphors. As I said, underlying

71

Happiness by Design and the whole idea of the pleasure–purpose principle is the basic conceptual metaphor that 'time is money': we spend, save or lose time, and so on. Everyone understands 'time is money' because it's one of the most common conceptual metaphors we have in the modern world. (After all, we sell our time for money in the process of labour.) So this makes Dolan's work instantly accessible simply because it rubs along the grain of what is so generally taken for granted. More fundamentally, because 'time is money' is linked to 'people are tools' and 'measuring everything for its use', it makes the book more coherent: for Dolan as for Gradgrind, 'every inch of the existence of mankind, from birth to death' is a financial transaction, 'a bargain across a counter'. Metaferocity is at work. A literary approach – reading closely, looking at the metaphors – acknowledges this and might lead a reader to ask: do we accept that basic metaphor? Is life like money? Our view on this influences how closely we follow what the implied Dolan says about happiness. We might choose to use or inhabit another basic conceptual metaphor, for example, or believe that we can have different understandings of attention. For the implied Dolan, attention is the currency we use to buy happiness. For the strange and beautiful thinker Simone Weil, in contrast, 'attention is the rarest and purest form of generosity'[35] and 'presupposes faith and love.'[36]

The implied Dolan likes useful things and dislikes useless ones. And yet he has to use what he thinks is useless (literature, the telling of silly stories, the tricks he doesn't approve of) to show us what he thinks is useful (the idea that time is money, for example). So while his book *tells* us that literature is useless, it actually *shows* us that literature is useful, more useful than anything else. (Seeing his book in this way is inspired by a critical method called 'deconstruction', which pays close attention to language and to what we actually say, as opposed to what we think we are saying.)

The implied Dolan might have a couple of objections to this. First, he might say: literature is fiction; it is untrue, made-up stories. But as I showed in chapter 1, 'fiction' doesn't really mean false: it means 'shaped' or 'formed'. Fictions are – exactly as Dolan says – 'made up' or shaped from things in the world: the story of his stutter is not false but 'made up', shaped in a certain way to make us feel sympathy for him; the journey we take through the book to understand the pleasure–purpose principle is formed; the body-building metaphor that beefs up *Happiness by Design* is designed. Second, he might say that this book was aimed at the 'general reader': his *real* work is made up of psychological articles published in scientific journals, written in a specialized language (although they are still full of tropes). But here again, the point is that when the implied Dolan seeks to write to join the wider human conversation ('for the general reader') he uses literature – precisely because it is, metaphorically, that living conversation.

Loving literature is not about boasting that you have read a novel; nor is hating literature crowing that you haven't (or that you've only read John Steinbeck's *Of Mice and Men*). Because literature and its study are like our conversation about ourselves, they flow out from books into everyday life, into everything. It is our inner culture, our ability to talk with ourselves and others, and our creation of meaning – exactly the pleasure and purpose Dolan discusses – in the world. And the implied Dolan, without knowing or admitting it, seems to have a lot of time for literature. So rather than turning his head from the conversation, perhaps he might enjoy it.

I wonder why the implied Dolan thinks what he does about literature. He writes that he is a neophile, he likes new things: one of his misunderstandings of literature seems to be that all novels are like the single novel he read at school. As I said in the first chapter, literature is not all one kind (you might even say: literature is not 'literature'): like a conversation, it is about all kinds of things and in different forms. Literature is always new; there are always new things to read or discover. Perhaps – recalling Mill – Dolan hasn't found his Wordsworth yet. Some people are grabbed by J. K. Rowling's stories of wizards; others prefer Jacqueline Wilson's gritty novels about broken homes and children in care. And sometimes, as I mentioned in chapter 1, literature needs 'attunement'. To use a metaphor the implied Dolan might appreciate: when you first go to the gym, you don't begin by trying to lift your own bodyweight or run 10k on a treadmill. You work and get used to the exercise; you gradually improve and attune your body. The study of literature needs attunement, which, like going to the gym, can be hard. Its growth is a process: like a conversation, you have to join in to help uncover its purpose for you. This process relies on a trust that something will emerge. (And – spoiler alert! – Gradgrind, a version of Scrooge, learns to trust and changes very profoundly over the course of *Hard Times*.)

Conclusion

This book has argued that literature can't be defined, and that this is part of its and our 'non-thinginess'. But any account of 'why literature matters', even one as broad and generous as suggesting that it triggers 'access to felt experience at the human core' and offers a 'freer, deeper and more mobile way of thinking', is going to tend towards a kind of definition or limitation. Does the poem 'Lines on the Antiquity of Microbes' by Strickland Gillilan (1869–1954) access the human core? Judge for yourself. Here it is, the whole poem: 'Adam/Had 'em'. I'm unsure: perhaps – because it's funny – it does? Perhaps, because it's only clever and funny, it doesn't? Either way, this chapter has chosen to explore in detail only one way in which literature matters to people, using the work of literary critics like Jane Davis and the psychologists of the Reader project. And then, using the work of another psychologist as an example of an anti-literary instrumentalism, I've shown not only that literature is useful, but also that it's everywhere. In the next chapter, I want to argue that not only is reading literature wonderful and useful, as the Reader project shows, but that its study is too.

4

What Does Literature Teach?

In the previous chapter, I argued that one way of thinking about why literature matters was because, as the report I cited said, 'what literature can do above all is (1) trigger access to felt experience at the human core and (2) offer a freer, deeper and more mobile way of thinking about it'.[1] I suggested that literature was where the reality that we are not machines or tools, not mere instruments, is made clear. And these are the heart of what literature teaches.

But, with an irony that Mr Gradgrind might not appreciate, this is why English and literary studies – and the humanities in general – provide an outstanding training for the world of work, precisely because we are not robots but people. Students are often told that to succeed in their careers they have to study science, technology, engineering and maths (the STEM subjects), but this is so simplistic as just not to be true. But you needn't believe me, google it. Or, rather, believe one of the world's largest technology employers, Google.

Cathy Davidson, in her book *The New Education: How to Revolutionize the University to Prepare Students for a World in Flux*, explains. In 2013, Google launched Project Oxygen: 'the most thorough, data-intensive study that any company has undertaken to understand the qualities that lead to promotion and a successful career'.[2] While Google's founders, Sergey Brin and Larry Page, began by thinking that only those with technological skills could succeed in a technological business, Project Oxygen discovered quite the opposite. The top six skills for success turned out to be 'being a good coach; communicating and listening well; possessing insights into others (including others' different values and points of view); having empathy toward and being supportive of one's colleagues; being a good critical thinker and problem solver; and being able to make connections across complex ideas'.[3] And, as Davidson says, these traits sound like what you learn studying literature rather than coding: 'STEM expertise without any grounding in interpretive and critical thinking skills may get you a first job, but it won't get you promoted'.[4] Google's next project focused on how teams work best,

[handwritten margin note: Sharing ideas / discussion / when learning lit]

and discovered that the 'company's most important and productive new ideas' came not from the technologists, but from the teams who felt secure and emotionally safe with each other, and who exhibited 'equality, generosity, curiosity toward the ideas of ... teammates, empathy, and emotional intelligence'. 'To succeed,' Davidson writes, 'each and every team member must feel confident speaking up and making mistakes. They must know they are being heard.'[5] Learning to have a real conversation together leads to success. Google projects are not alone: research shows unambiguously that companies big and small value and are looking for skills in communication, collaboration, critical thinking, independence and adaptability.

Maybe this all sounds a bit 'gradgrindy', but if you're investing your time, money and future in a subject, it's fine to be a little hard-headed. And perhaps the risk of sounding like Mr Gradgrind has meant that people in English and literary studies haven't always been so good at promoting this aspect of the subject. But what you learn from English, both at the profoundest level and at the level of skills, is useful for society as well as for yourself. The bottom line is: employers love English and literary studies and it's important to explain why. So here is a list of skills that the UK Government's

What Does Literature Teach?

Qualifications Assurance Agency says that you will learn if you study literature (over and above your knowledge and understanding of literature and ideas):

You will be an effective researcher: able to discover and synthesize complex information and diverse evidence; respond creatively and imaginatively to research tasks. You will be able to initiate projects of your own. You will be able to present information within wider contexts, test, interpret and analyse information and evidence independently and critically, producing from that analysis cogent arguments and decisive judgements and plan, organize and report to deadline.

You will be a *good communicator* possessing advanced communication skills and able to articulate your own and other people's ideas concisely, accurately and persuasively both orally and in writing. You will develop working relationships with others in teams, especially through constructive dialogue (for example, by listening, asking and responding to questions). You will understand the role of narrative and emotion in decision-making.

You will become an *active, lifelong learner* who can adapt to different demands and tasks, appreciate the benefit of giving and receiving feedback, evaluate and reflect on your own practices and assumptions, look beyond the immediate task to

the wider context, including the social and commercial effects of your work and initiate and take responsibility for your own work.[6] *I context i
shey*

To be honest, put like this, because they are stripped of their context, these skills sound deadly dull, but interestingly, this dullness teaches us something important. You can only learn skills in a context, or, as the jargon has it, 'embedded' in undertaking an activity. Just as you can only learn to swim in water, you learn to be a communicator in and through communicating in a seminar. You learn to initiate a project by developing and following your interest in kingship in Shakespeare *or* British Muslim women *learning confider* writers *or* homosexual desire in nineteenth-century fiction *or* . . . any of the infinite things that grab you *talking* about literature. You learn to manage your time *about* (however often you are told about how to do this) *Puss* by actually managing it yourself in your researching, planning, writing and giving in(!) an essay. These skills are learned in one context and then can be transferred into another.

This 'embeddedness' means that the word 'skills' isn't quite the right one. In terms of education, we can learn simple skills by ourselves: for example, you can learn the names of different tropes from a book (although it's more fun doing it together), *long-term skill.*

just as you can learn to cook a particular dish from watching YouTube. But learning to be good at a shared activity, or learning to be good at discussing and thinking through things with others, is different. You can only do it *with* others and so need to learn how to do it with others. Again: you can learn to kick a ball accurately, or memorize lines from a play by yourself. But you can only learn to play well in a team, or act well on stage with others. If studying literature is like a conversation, it must, as all conversations do, involve others.

it and discussion not in a vacuum

So it's significant how many of the 'skills' in the Qualifications Assurance Agency's benchmarking statement for English are a mixture of 'skills' and 'activities'. Responding creatively and imaginatively to others; working and communicating; reasoning and deliberating; developing relationships; adapting to different tasks; taking responsibility: all these are skills in the broadest sense, of course, but they are also shared actions. They can only be done with others. This is exactly why an English or literary studies degree can't be learned from a book, or from an online course: what it teaches comes in no small part from interactions with others at a complex level. It is precisely because English graduates are good at communal activity that employers want them. Davidson again: 'STEM skills are vital to the world we live in today, but technology alone, as Steve Jobs famously insisted, is not enough. We desperately need the expertise of those who are educated to the human, cultural, and social as well as the computational.'[7] What you learn as a student of literature is vital for the world and the workplace, because our shared world depends exactly on what the study of literature requires: the manipulation and understanding of symbols, words, stories, or, more widely, our human conversation. In these times of fake news and media manipulation, these are of ever greater importance. These skills and a growing expertise in shared activities are not added on to the delight you might get from reading and talking about literature; they come from exactly that access to 'the human core' and 'freer, deeper and more mobile way of thinking' that literature offers.

If You Study Literature, What Do You Become?

In the rest of this chapter, I want to argue that in addition to the acquisition of skills there is an even deeper benefit from the study of literature. This reason is important yet often passed over, in part because literary studies is sometimes bad at making a case for itself, fearing Mr Gradgrind, and in part because it's complicated to explain but actually actually quite straightforward. It also has significant consequences for how we understand the study of literature.

Studying doesn't just add skills, as if you were downloading apps to a phone. Rather, it changes *who you are*. It literally changes your identity. You can hear this in everyday speech. If you study maths, you learn to think like – you *are* – a mathematician. If you study history, you learn to think like – you *become* – a historian. And if you study English . . . ? Literary studies . . . ?

By using the metaphor of conversation, I've stressed the dialogical nature of both literature and literary studies. I think that this is the best way, too, of understanding what a degree in English or in literary studies offers: a chance to join the conversation of our species. In this, you don't only explore and deepen what you think, pay attention to and learn from what others think, but you also come to discover what people over a longer period have thought and felt, what people think and feel now, and you learn to be open to what people will think and feel in the future. Perhaps in physics, it doesn't really matter what scientists thought fifty years ago: it's out of date. But generally in the humanities, the

[handwritten annotation: → how you look at past to understand how]

conversation is rooted in and through our engagement with the past, present and future, and the
people who work in a field interpret this. They are
an 'interpretive community'.

This phrase comes from the American critic
Stanley Fish. He worked on John Milton's epic
seventeenth-century poem *Paradise Lost*. An epic
poem usually tells the story of the foundation or
life-or-death struggle of a state, a city: some huge
(epic!) event. *Paradise Lost* is the story of what
Milton (1608–74) took to be the foundation of
all humankind: Adam and Eve, tempted by Satan,
and their fall from the Garden of Eden. Since its
first publication in 1667, readers have been puz-
zled by the way that Satan, the ultimate figure of
evil, is given so many admirable characteristics: he
is heroic, eloquent, determined, charismatic, convincing. He's so heroic that the south London poet
William Blake (1757–1827) wrote – in a line that
has been churned out in untold millions of essay
questions – that 'Milton was of the devil's party
without knowing it'. However, in 1967, Stanley
Fish joined this conversation by arguing that this
was part of the point of *Paradise Lost*: we, the readers, are supposed to find Satan heroic, daring and
persuasive precisely to warn us that these qualities
– so well exemplified by the figure of absolute

[handwritten annotation: makes the reader understand the story knowing the moral]

evil – are not to be trusted.[8] The controversy his argument stirred up led Fish to think about how and why books are interpreted in different ways. He suggested that there is a very roughly defined 'interpretive community' of those who have similar ideas about and ways of interpreting texts. These communities vary in size: you and your friends share an in-joke that others can't understand; one generation uses a phrase ('CBA'; 'tl;dr') that older (and younger) people can't follow; a community of literary critics follow a certain (hard to define) set of ideas when reading texts. For Fish, new inter-pretations evolve by using the rules in new ways, or – more often – through changing the rules of interpretation themselves. Indeed, the more open any interpretive community is, the easier it is to change the rules.[9] (You can see that this idea is akin to the idea of genre, which I discussed in chapter 1. If, in the genre of detective fiction, the rule is that the detective is strong and quick, you can challenge this rule, and shift the genre by inventing a fat, slow detective. But would a story about a fictional detec-tive who instead of solving crimes swanned about falling in love be detective fiction? Genres – and interpretive communities – have their limits.)

[handwritten annotation: each generation; bring personal element]

Interpretive communities are made up of both ideas (about, for example, what literature is) and practices (say: the practice of close reading; thinking about the role played by basic conceptual metaphors). Joining the conversation means learning to become part of a developing interpretive community. I think of this as coming to take on a 'disciplinary consciousness' because in joining a community you learn an identity, you learn a way of thinking. Geography makes geographers; psychology psychologists. These forms of identity are pretty strong (one famous study calls them 'tribes'[10]).

The name for the interpretive community for English is ... well, that's not so straightforward. To explain why it's complicated, and what this means for our interpretive community, involves a swift detour through the past, present and future of the conversation of literary studies to (very quickly) explain how we got here and where we might be going.

Literary Studies in the Past

Towards the end of the nineteenth century, four different strands of what we think of as literary studies began to weave together. The reason this early part of the conversation is important is that – as in any conversation – literary studies is rooted in these ideas and they still play some role in how the subject is studied.

One strand of this conversation was the subject called *philology,* the 'king of the sciences, the pride of the first great modern universities'.[11] Philology, which flourished in the eighteenth and early nineteenth centuries, marked the beginning of the modern humanities, and involved the study of texts, languages and speculation about the origins of language itself. (The author of *The Lord of the Rings*, J. R. R. Tolkien was a philologist, and his fictional world grew out of his interest in the history of languages: he invented, first, a fictional language for elves, and then grew a world and mythology for this language to describe.) The study of English language inherits some aspects of philology. Another part of this conversation was the subject of *rhetoric*: teaching people to write, to speak and to argue well; the study of composition stems, in part, from this. The third strand of conversation was the more informal discussions of literature undertaken as much by poets, novelists, teachers and academics and others in magazines and newspapers in the second half of the nineteenth century: this is often called *belles lettres*, beautiful writing. And finally towards the end of the nineteenth century in the UK, there was a huge growth in adult education. University was expensive and just for the very privileged; yet there was a growing interest in reading and discussing literary works. This was met by 'extra-mural' classes (literally, 'outside the walls' of the universities). Adults took these classes not for exams or qualifications but for their own self-improvement, and historians are coming to see the importance of the *literary educators* who led these classes. (I mentioned one of these, Richard Moulton, in chapter 2.) All these strands combined with strong forms of nationalism, both within the then United Kingdom (in relation especially to Scotland, Wales and Ireland) and its wider colonies, especially India, to establish a subject for which national identity became central: English was about being, or becoming, English.[12]

However, it wasn't until after the First World War that English became fully established in universities and, in this process, it underwent a sea change through a special and intense focus on literature itself. Philology seemed out of date, concerned with the history not the meaning of texts; rhetoric seemed interested in literature only for examples of how to write well; and 'belles-lettrism' seemed too individual, subjective and amateur. (In fact, of course, just as in a conversation, each of these strands had and has much of worth in them.) In their place there arose a new understanding of the idea of *literary criticism*.

What Does Literature Teach?

[handwritten margin note: learners deciding what to keep and change]

One crucial element of this was the work of T. S. Eliot. In a very famous essay, 'Tradition and the Individual Talent' (1919), he argued that literature could only really be produced and understood in relation to other literature: to become a writer, and by extension to understand a writer's work, meant understanding the tradition of writing. This idea is insightful: I suggested in chapter 1 that writers create through reading and responding to other writers, and that literature can be seen as a series of relationships. But the idea of tradition also suggests limitations: a tradition can imprison as well as liberate creativity, and writers and readers respond to more than just other literary texts. I. A. Richards' work was crucial for the growth of criticism. In chapter 2 I showed how he inspired critics like William Empson and Q. D. Leavis, who took the task of criticism very seriously and were also extremely significant in the UK; he was also one of the key influences on the New Critics in the USA. They taught students who went on to become teachers, in schools and universities, and so influenced several generations of literature students and scholars. For all these writers and teachers, criticism was a central term. Criticism was infused with the idea that English was itself a discipline of thought.

As this idea of criticism came to dominate the

study of literature, it became less like a constructive, open dialogue and more like a dominating voice
which refused to let others speak. Yet, in response
to the changing wider world in the 1960s, 1970s
and 1980s, and in antagonistic reaction to criticism, many new voices and approaches to literature
sought to be heard. Inspired by feminism, Marxism,
new perspectives on literature from philosophy,
science, sociology, history and psychoanalysis,
and ideas about race and empire, these new voices
became lumped together rather clumsily as 'theory'.
'Theorists' came to be seen to be opposed to critics. In
addition, theorists developed their own specialisms:
postcolonial theorists, who studied the relationship
between literature, the experience of empire, decolonization and our global world; feminist theorists,
who explored gender in writing; and psychoanalytic
critics, who developed the insights of Freud and
others in order to understand the psyche in culture.
The clash between theorists of different stripes and
critics meant that this period was called, rather mel-
odramatically, 'the culture wars' or 'theory wars'.

Literary Studies in the Present

Despite fiery critical debates, by the 1990s, and into
the new millennium, the 'culture wars' seemed to
be over. This was because many people in literary

studies were happy to let a thousand flowers bloom and found the discipline much wider and more open than it had been. However, more significantly, it was because a kind of criticism based on history was now in the ascendant. In response to the seemingly abstract, inaccessible and endless nature of some theoretical debate ('What *is* this book about?'), literary texts were read as both coming from and evidence about a historical period ('It is about *this* historical moment!'). History became the main source for the interpretation of literature. Historical information seems to offer an unassailable and certain interpretation of a text, with a catalogue of facts, in contrast to the more tentative results of a dialogical and open-ended approach. More, original historical documents as well as the works of history they inspire are texts that require interpretation rather than 'answers' to interpretation. In universities, people became increasingly defined by the period they researched and taught: 'Renaissance' or 'Modernist' specialists, for example. Just as theorists had supplanted critics, so *cultural historians* supplanted theorists. In the present, too, we have access to the astonishing resources offered by the digital age. In this, as I've suggested, huge amounts of text can be 'read' by computers, resulting in new forms of knowledge about how literature was consumed, written and understood in the past. This approach, using the capabilities of computation, many of them as yet undiscovered, is known as the *digital humanities*. It, too, is often a kind of cultural history. At the far end of this spectrum are people who study not literature, but how literature was and is delivered: the history of the book. For these *historians of the book*, it's not the literary text that is important, or the debates about it, but the material form in which it exists.

Literary Studies in the Future

The conversation of literary studies does not end here. Three current trends, for example, might give new answers to what you become if you study literature.

First, creative writing has now become, and will continue to be, a major and growing part of literary studies. Creative writing focuses directly on the creative response to literary works and does not supplant what has gone before but builds on it: as Stephen King showed, *creative writers* are always creative readers, too. Creative writing is a form of criticism with a special interest in seeing an artwork from the point of view of the artist.

Second, the huge growth in the study of children's and young adult (YA) fiction is a response

[handwritten margin notes: "relevant", "to age and experience"]

to the 'golden age' of this genre in which we are living. It is part of the longer investigation of the special intertwining of literature and the development of the sense of a self. It also stems from the feeling people have that they *own* YA fiction, and so can engage in a proper, real dialogue about it. For example, many students of English have grown up with, lived with, *Harry Potter*, and so, when it comes to discussing it in seminars, they feel expert and confident: they *own* these texts in a powerful and rewarding way and so their dialogue with them is less inhibited by, for example, 'catalogues of information' downloaded into them.

Finally, there is a multi-billion dollar computer game industry that relies on many of the same qualities as literature: narrative, immersion, beauty, enjoyment. Games are now sophisticated works of art, not only in how they look and how they play – their 'ludic' element – but in their narratives and possibilities, too. Like novels, they can be immersive; like literature, they beg questions and require interpretations. For example, *Skyrim* (2011) is characterized by interlocking narratives and major existential personal and political decisions. *Red Dead Redemption* (2010) juxtaposes moments of outstanding beauty and contemplation with corruption, violence and a kind of knee-jerk

[handwritten margin note: "developing story"]

anti-government politics; indeed, this juxtaposition is the theme of the game. Many players remember the long ride along the southern bank side of the Rio Grande, enforced by the game mechanics, as an emotional high point. The sudden ending of the game, after a long section of bucolic play, is especially poignant. And while the violence, sexism and right-wing anti-politics of Rockstar's other enormous franchise, *Grand Theft Auto* (*GTA*), have (rightly, in my view) attracted criticism, the complex character interplay in *GTA V* (2013) between Michael De Santa, Trevor Philips and Franklin Clinton is often ignored. Michael seems a loving family man, certainly, but he is also untrustworthy and selfish; Trevor is notoriously violent and drunken, but loyal to a fault, determined and meticulous; Franklin, the character who has apparently least to lose and the most to gain, the most alienated from the world, is the central and generous moral compass of *GTA*. In stark contrast to the politics of *GTA*, *This War of Mine* (2016) is inspired by the siege of Sarajevo and is about the grim and distressing experience of civilians attempting to survive in a war zone. I've had long and literary conversations with all sorts of people about games of this sort. Critical terms are emerging around games: 'ludo-narrative dissonance', for example, describes the difference between how a game plays and the story it tells (you may play a character as evil, yet the game storyline means he or she is treated as a hero; the character may be supposed to be peace-loving but is a skilled warrior when you control them). There is no name yet for this kind of literary-inspired analysis of games, which often occurs on YouTube channels: *ludo-criticism,* perhaps.

All three of these future trends share something in common. The reader (as writer, as gamer) has a sense of personal engagement and dialogue with the texts and with others.

Crisis? Criticism!

In this much too brief history of the past, present and possible futures of literary studies you can trace the changing names for this interpretive community: philologists, rhetoricians, belle-lettrists, literary critics, theorists, cultural historians, digital humanists, historians of the book, creative writers, YA critics, ludo-critics. (It's missed out a lot, too: among many omissions, there are *comparativists*, who study the relationship of the literature of different nations; and there is the discipline of *cultural studies*, which grew from literary studies to analyse many wider forms of cultural production.) Each name emphasizes a different aspect of the study of literature. I think that this is probably healthy and right. A discipline based on something that can't be defined, an interpretive community based on a living conversation, should be open-ended, engaged in a debate about its nature, unclear quite what it is called. If this sounds a bit like a crisis, then it's a healthy one.

However, it's obvious, too, that a subject needs a name; it needs 'something' one becomes. So I think it is time to reclaim the phrase 'literary critic' for the identity for the subject. *If you study literature, you become a literary critic.* Indeed, 'critic' and 'crisis' have the same etymological root in Classical Greek.

To call people who study literature *critics* is not to hark back to some time 'before theory', before feminism and all the other social, political and intellectual concerns that theory embodied; nor to ignore cultural history; nor to insist on a focus on art for art's sake; nor to demand that studying literary texts is about explicitly evaluating them. Instead, criticism names a very broad, capacious field, which, like the literature it examines, is open to a huge range of influences: political, artistic, histori-cal, cultural and philosophical. Although criticism is no longer principally evaluative, it cannot escape

seeing a text in a wider context.

wider questions about value (to choose one book to read or teach or write about over another is a form of evaluation, after all). To reclaim criticism is to escape the idea that theory or cultural history marked a sort of 'year zero' which wiped out everything before it and develop a longer and wider sense of conversation.

Criticism in this capacious sense suggests that a subject is an evolving conversation. As I suggested in chapter 1, integral to a healthy conversation is a debate and discussion about how that conversation works, what motivates it, its continuities and discontinuities and how it can change. Everyone involved in – or who wants to be involved in – that conversation should have access to those debates. The term 'criticism' need not imply that there is some kind of core or essential strand to literary studies. Indeed, seeing 'criticism' as an evolving conversation means that people do not need all to agree on a common core that 'is' criticism: we can pursue a multi-vocal developing conversation.

Thinking of the subject as criticism, too, confronts one of the problems with literary studies. Sometimes it can look like 'just reading books'. It is more than this – it is an interpretive community. It is made up of a set of questions, ideas and approaches that structure and inform these readings. Thinking

Correct attitude.

about the discipline a little in this historical sense offers a way of bringing this important aspect to the fore. One of the most important elements in pedagogy is what's called 'metacognition', which means, roughly, knowing why you are studying something: if you know *why* you are studying something, or why you are studying in that way, the subject becomes easier to understand and you become better at it. Just giving a name to an activity does not explain it, but it does give it a sense of direction.

The name 'criticism' draws attention to the practice of the subject, how it is actually done. Practices – as the practice of close reading shows – often survive changes of emphasis and name. For example, in relation to writing and assessment, generally students do not write sonnets or five-act tragedies. They write works of criticism, responding to the texts in ways that we recognize as 'literary critical'. Thinking as critics means that students of literature do not only read works of literature but can also see that the works of criticism they read are there as part of a continuum to help them learn to be writers and critics themselves. Recent developments in writing – creative writing or creative critical rewriting, for example – support this enlarged idea of criticism: these are now part of our critical repertoire (and perhaps coding and critical game design in the future might become so?).

The idea of becoming a critic through studying literature also gives balance to the idea of assessment objectives. All examining and assessment involves a certain amount of 'hoop-jumping', but sometimes the assessment objectives can make reading and writing into a 'tick-box' exercise (and the examining system can exacerbate this). Assessment objectives are not supposed be hoops or boxes, however; rather they are a necessarily clumsy encoding of the sort of questions critics ask. They are supposed to be an indication of the route to follow, the ideas that form a critic's identity, ways to help you join the conversation. When they become tick-boxes rather than directions, they have lost their dialogical function.

Criticism is a collective activity, shared between people, arising out of conversation, argument, shared thought. The American critic Wayne Booth wrote about the activity of criticism not as induction or deduction, but as 'co-duction', 'a process that is not mere argument for views already established, but a conversation, a kind of rereading that is an essential part of what will be a kind of continually shifting evaluation'.[13] We develop ideas about literature together: one can talk, read, work with

[handwritten margin notes: "not simply creative receptive", "not creative"]

[handwritten note at bottom: "learning what came before and adding own understanding"]

100

others, doing criticism as a collaboration which – like a healthy democracy – takes regard of others but does not necessarily require total agreement. This collaboration can also be seen to work over time: debates and arguments over what *King Lear* is about can shift and change, and in this way a student today can learn from critics in the past.

This sense of criticism, too, teaches us something important. Criticism, like conversation, includes disagreement, but people can disagree as critics and still inhabit the same conversation. In this way, criticism is a model for democracy in our increasingly polarized world. Criticism does not just belong in universities, but seen like this, you can see why it flourishes in that environment. Universities are places that grow and preserve the many ecosystems that are disciplinary interpretive communities. Many of these reach beyond the university (some more than others), but the university has a duty to preserve the range of intellectual biodiversity.

The term 'criticism', too, also carries a warning. Sometimes a sense of identity can get in the way: recall how Jane Davis wrote that 'without the screen of "teaching", without "University course", without "classroom", the stuff of feeling was exposed as live ammunition'. The implication is that the 'interpretive community' can obstruct rather than

approach and attitude

enhance how we encounter literature. This is true at all levels of the subject: think about how reading a novel for pleasure can differ from reading a novel for an essay. Notice, too, how the various waves that make up the discipline of literary studies keep trying, through their arguments with each other, to find their way back to something ('something else', we might say). And there can sometimes be a tension between, on the one hand, the concrete objectives of obtaining skills and qualifications and, on the other, a more intangible but still real sense of individual and communal betterment. Literary studies is right at this point of tension because it is about deeply significant things – personal response and experience, beauty, passion, interest, otherness, community, delight – which are all really hard to pin down for an exam. Being a literature student involves 'living through' this tension, to find, ide-ally, ways in which it is productive: where, say, your passion for a writer leads you to do your very best, most interesting work.

each respon will vary based on experience

Finally, and to return to where this chapter began, to the question of skills and the world of work, criticism answers the question of what you become if you study literature. As I suggested above, study-ing doesn't just add skills: it changes *who you are*, your identity. You grasp a disciplinary consciousness. When you know how a subject works – what the questions are and why, what counts as a proper answer and how it came to be that way – you have grasped it: you have understood the rules of that interpretive community. This is crucial for the world of work. Once you have learned the rules of one interpretive community, it's much easier to learn the rules of another because you know what it's like to master something, to understand why. Learning to become a literary critic means that it's easier to learn to become something else. In the world of work today, jobs are constantly changing and developing. New ideas, practices and technologies will shape future careers and identities. In this sense, learning the open-ended rules of one interpretive community means you can learn others: you know what counts and why. Students of literature learn their disciplinary consciousness by reading and discussing novels, poems, plays, other texts and works of criticism, theory and history. As this book has argued, the 'disciplinary consciousness' of criticism is – or should be – open-ended, reflective and open to new ideas: this is crucial in learning how to learn for life.

If you are studying literature, you have to enjoy reading, because that's the main thing you'll be doing. You have to be keen to be able to study

[handwritten marginal note: Teaches adaptation]

independent study.
guided study.

independently. Literary students don't go to labs all day; instead, with support from their tutors, lectures and seminars, they read, explore, research by themselves or in small groups. And you have to enjoy communicating – talking, writing, joking, arguing and trying to say what you think about writers and critics. You have to be willing to take intellectual risks, to try new texts, new approaches and to be open-minded about new possibilities in the conversation.

Conclusion

This chapter has argued that as well as what Jane Davis called the 'something else', that profound orientation towards what it is to exist and to experience the world, the study of literature provides an array of crucial skills for the workplace. More, if you come to understand one especially reflective interpretive community, then you also come to understand what it means to become proficient in another. On our rapidly changing globe, nobody should feel that the pressure of earning a living should stop them studying literature: what you learn from your conversation with literature will enable you to join the conversation of the world.

Notes

Chapter 1 What is Literature?

1 Laurie Anderson, *United States* (New York: Harper & Row, 1984).

2 Alan Bennett, *The History Boys* (London: Faber & Faber, 2004), p. 56.

3 William Shakespeare, *Hamlet* II.2.

4 Terry Eagleton, *How to Read Literature* (New Haven, CT: Yale University Press, 2013), p. 192.

5 Doris Lessing, 'Preface', in *The Golden Notebook* (London: HarperCollins, 2007), p. 18.

6 Virginia Woolf, 'George Eliot', *Times Literary Supplement*, 20 November, 1919.

7 George Eliot, *Middlemarch* (London: Penguin, 1994), p. 164.

8 Wai Chee Dimock, *Through Other Continents: American Literature across Deep Time* (Princeton, NJ: Princeton University Press, 2006), p. 4.

9 Lessing, 'Preface', pp. 17–18.

10 Salman Rushdie, *Step across This Line: Collected*

Non-Fiction 1992–2002 (London: Vintage, 2003), p. 232.

11 Czesław Miłosz, 'Ars Poetica?', trans. Czesław Miłosz and Lillian Vallee (https://www.poetryfoundation.org/poems/49455/ars-poetica-56d22b8f31558).

Chapter 2 Studying Literature

1 Maggie Zhang, '22 Lessons from Stephen King on How to be a Great Writer', *Independent*, 26 October 2017 (https://www.independent.co.uk/arts-entertainment/books/news/stephen-king-22-lessons-creative-writing-advice-novels-short-stories-a8021511.html).

2 Not an entirely unwarranted analogy: we *play* a sport, we *play* as children, we joke around or make memes using 'word*play*', we go to see a *play* performed . . .

3 Ben Knights, *Pedagogic Criticism: Reconfiguring University English Studies* (London: Palgrave Macmillan, 2017), p. 1.

4 According to a Royal Society of Literature report in 2017, 75 per cent of adults in the UK have read a work they consider literature in the last six months: *Literature in Britain Today* (https://rsliterature.org/wp-content/uploads/2017/02/RSL-Literature-in-Britain-Today_01.03.17.pdf).

5 T. S. Eliot, 'The Perfect Critic', in *Selected Prose*, ed. Frank Kermode (London: Faber & Faber, 1975), p. 55.

6 Jodie Archer and Matthew L. Jockers, *The Bestseller*

Code: Anatomy of the Blockbuster Novel (London: St Martin's Press, 2016), p. 188. For more on neurosciences and literature, see Lisa Zunshine, ed., *The Oxford Handbook of Cognitive Literary Studies* (Oxford: Oxford University Press, 2015).

7 John Crowe Ransom, 'Criticism, Inc.', *VQR* (Autumn 1937) (https://www.vqronline.org/essay/criticism-inc-0).

8 M. M. Bakthin, *The Dialogic Imagination*, ed. Michael Holquist, trans. Caryl Emerson and Michael Holquist (Austin: University of Texas Press, 1981). A good account is Ken Hischkop, *Mikhail Bakhtin: An Aesthetic for Democracy* (Oxford: Oxford University Press, 2002), and a good introduction to his thought is Alastair Renfrew, *Mikhail Bahktin* (London: Routledge, 2015).

9 F. R. Leavis, *The Common Pursuit* (London: Penguin Books, 1952), p. 1. Simon During's chapter 'When Literary Criticism Mattered', in Rónán McDonald, ed., *The Values of Literary Studies* (Cambridge: Cambridge University Press, 2015), is an excellent discussion of the Leavises, and there is a very good biography of F. R. Leavis: Ian MacKillop, *F. R. Leavis: A Life in Criticism* (London: Penguin, 1997). Richard Storer, *F. R. Leavis* (London: Routledge, 2009), is an excellent introduction.

10 Paulo Freire, *Pedagogy of the Oppressed*, trans. Myra Bergman Ramos (New York: Continuum, 1997), p. 54.

11 Ibid., p. 70.

12 Ibid., p. 69.

13 On this see, amongst others, Antonia Darder, *Reinventing Paulo Freire*, 2nd edn (London: Routledge, 2017).

14 Arthur N. Applebee, *Curriculum as Conversation: Transforming Traditions of Teaching and Learning* (Chicago: University of Chicago Press, 1996), p. 90.

15 Ibid., p. 91.

16 Sappho, 'Fragment 31', trans. Julia Dubnoff (http://www.uh.edu/~cldue/texts/sappho.html). Read the rest, it will only take ten minutes.

17 George Lakoff and Mark Johnson, *Metaphors We Live By* (Chicago: University of Chicago Press, 2003). In addition, and in this context, see also George Lakoff and Mark Turner, *More Than Cool Reason: A Field Guide to Poetic Metaphor* (Chicago: University of Chicago Press, 1989).

18 Daniel Dennett, *Consciousness Explained* (London: Penguin, 1991), p. 455.

19 Sappho, 'Fragment 11', trans. Julia Dubnoff (as note 16). That's the whole fragment, by the way.

20 Barbara Herrnstein Smith, 'What Was "Close Reading"'? A Century of Method in Literary Studies', *Minnesota Review* 87 (2016), p. 57.

21 This story, with Richards' comments, is retold in John Haffenden, *William Empson, Volume 1: Among the Mandarins* (Oxford: Oxford University Press, 2005), p. 207.

22 William Empson, *Seven Types of Ambiguity* (London: Penguin Books, 1995), p. 19.

23 Michael Wood, *On Empson* (Princeton, NJ: Princeton University Press, 2017), p. 47.

24 See Alexandra Lawrie, *The Beginnings of University English: Extramural Study 1885–1910* (London: Palgrave Macmillan, 2014), pp. 93ff.
25 Terry Eagleton, *How to Read a Poem* (Oxford: Blackwell, 2007), p. 9.
26 On all this, see also Harold Rosen's lecture, 'Neither *Bleak House* nor *Liberty Hall*: English in the Curriculum', in John Richmond, ed., *Harold Rosen: Writings on Life, Language and Learning 1958 to 2008* (London: Institute of Education Press, 2017).

Chapter 3 Why Does Literature Matter?

1 Jane Davis, 'Something Real to Carry Home When Day is Done', in Gail Marshall and Robert Eaglestone, eds, *English: Shared Futures* (Woodbridge: Boydell & Brewer, 2018), p. 211.
2 You can read this Wordsworth poem here: https://www.poetryfoundation.org/poems/45536/ode-intimations-of-immortality-from-recollections-of-early-childhood.
3 Davis, 'Something Real to Carry Home', p. 212.
4 *Crossing the Bar*

> Sunset and evening star,
>   And one clear call for me!
> And may there be no moaning of the bar,
>   When I put out to sea,
>
> But such a tide as moving seems asleep,
>   Too full for sound and foam,
> When that which drew from out the boundless deep
>   Turns again home.

> Twilight and evening bell,
>> And after that the dark!
> And may there be no sadness of farewell,
>> When I embark;
>
> For tho' from out our bourne of Time and Place
>> The flood may bear me far,
> I hope to see my Pilot face to face
>> When I have crost the bar.

5 Davis, 'Something Real to Carry Home', pp. 213–14.

6 This is the Reader project's website: http://www. thereader.org.uk/. Go and look.

7 Philip Davis, Fiona Magee, Kremena Koleva, Thor Magnus Tangeras, Elisabeth Hill, Helen Baker and Laura Crane (2016), *What Literature Can Do: An Investigation into the Effectiveness of Shared Reading as a Whole Population Health Intervention* (University of Liverpool, 2016) (http://www.threa der.org.uk/literature-can-investigation-effectiveness-shared-reading-whole-population-health-interventio n/), p. 9.

8 Ibid., p. 19.

9 Ibid., p. 25.

10 Ibid., p. 47.

11 Ibid., p.57.

12 Charles Dickens, *Hard Times* (Harmondsworth: Penguin, 1969), p. 47.

13 Freire, *Pedagogy of the Oppressed*, p. 53.

14 Dickens, *Hard Times*, p. 48.

15 Ibid., p. 304.

16 Jeremy Bentham, *The Rationale of Reward* (London: John and H. L. Hunt, 1827), p. 206.

17 This and all other quotations from John Stuart Mill are from *Autobiography*, ch. 5. This text is available online at Project Gutenberg: http://www.gutenberg.org/ebooks/10378.

18 See *Memoirs of Marmontel Written by Himself*, Vol. 1 (https://archive.org/details/memoirsmarmonte 01marmgoog), pp. 49–51.

19 Paul Dolan, *Happiness by Design: Finding Pleasure and Purpose in Everyday Life* (London: Penguin, 2014), p. 10.

20 Ibid.

21 Ibid., p. xviii.

22 Ibid., p. xix.

23 Ibid., p. xi.

24 Ibid., p. 152.

25 Ibid., p. 177.

26 Ibid., p. 182.

27 'Happiness Expert Paul Dolan: What Makes Me Happy', *Guardian*, 22 November 2014 (https://www.theguardian.com/lifeandstyle/2014/nov/22/happiness-expert-paul-dolan-what-makes-me-happy). The following Dolan quotations, unless noted otherwise, are from this newspaper profile.

28 Dolan, *Happiness by Design*, pp. 80–1.

29 Ibid., p. 140.

30 Ibid., p. 181.

31 Ibid., p. 189.

32 Ibid., p. 46.

33 Ibid., p. 52.

34 Ibid., pp. 15, 194.

35 Simone Weil, letter to Joë Bousquet, 13 April 1942, quoted in Simone Pétrement, *Simone Weil: A Life*, trans. Raymond Rosenthal (New York: Pantheon, 1976), p. 462.

36 Simone Weil, *Gravity and Grace*, trans. Emma Crawford and Mario von der Ruhr (London: Routledge, 2002), p. 117.

Chapter 4 What Does Literature Teach?

1 Davis et al., *What Literature Can Do*.

2 Cathy N. Davidson, *The New Education: How to Revolutionize the University to Prepare Students for a World in Flux* (New York: Basic Books, 2017), p. 140.

3 Cathy N. Davidson, 'The Surprising Thing Google Learned About Its Employees – and What It Means for Today's Students', *Washington Post*, 20 December 2017 (https://www.washingtonpost.com/news/answer-sheet/wp/2017/12/20/the-surprising-thing-google-learned-about-its-employees-and-what-it-means-for-todays-students/?utm_term=.f57494cc1785).

4 Davidson, *The New Education*, p. 140.

5 Davidson, 'The Surprising Thing'.

6 The document is here: http://www.qaa.ac.uk/docs/qaa/subject-benchmark-statements/sbs-english-15.pdf?sfvrsn=4f9df781_10. It's a bit dry, of course, but the crucial pages are 5–10. If you are doing a degree in English, this tells you what it should be like.

7 Davidson, 'The Surprising Thing'.

8 Stanley Fish, *Surprised by Sin* (Cambridge, MA: Harvard University Press, 1967).

9 Fish's idea of interpretive communities is outlined in Stanley Fish, *Is There a Text in This Class?* (Cambridge, MA: Harvard University Press, 1980).

10 Tony Becher and Paul Trowler, *Academic Tribes and Territories* (Maidenhead: Open University Press, 2001).

11 James Turner, *Philology: The Forgotten Origins of the Modern Humanities* (Princeton, NJ: Princeton University Press, 2014), p. x.

12 There are very many accounts of this history now. Three famous ones are: Chris Baldick, *The Social Mission of English Criticism, 1848–1932* (Oxford: Clarendon Press, 1983), which covers the UK; Gerald Graff, *Professing Literature: An Institutional History* (Chicago: University of Chicago Press, 2007), which covers the USA; and Gauri Viswanathan, *Masks of Conquest: Literary Study and British Rule in India* (New York: Columbia University Press, 1989), which focuses on the role of Empire in the establishment of the subject. Recent additions to the conversation are: Ted Underwood's historical overview *Why Literary Periods Mattered: Historical Contrast and the Prestige of English Studies* (Stanford: Stanford University Press, 2013); Carol Atherton, *Defining Literary Criticism* (Basingstoke: Macmillan, 2005), which is especially good on the way older debates still structure contemporary ideas; Michael Gardiner's polemical and forceful *The Constitution of English*

Literature: The State, the Nation and the Canon (London: Bloomsbury, 2013); Alexandra Lawrie, *The Beginnings of University English: Extramural Study 1885–1910* (London: Palgrave Macmillan, 2014), which explores the adult education movement; Deidre Shauna Lynch, *Loving Literature: A Cultural History* (Chicago: University of Chicago Press, 2015), which takes the evolution of the subject back to the eighteenth century; and Louis Menard, *The Marketplace of Ideas* (New York: W. W. Norton, 2010), which is funny and very readable.

13 Wayne C. Booth, *The Company We Keep: An Ethics of Fiction* (Berkeley: University of California Press, 1988), p. 75.

Further Reading

There are problems with a 'Further Reading' section in a book about literature. For a start, suggestions of books you *could* read often sound like instructions for books you *should* read, as I discussed in chapter 1. Second, and as Doris Lessing pointed out, you never quite know if it's the right time in your life to read something someone recommends. And finally, new literature is being written and old literature rediscovered all the time. While writing this book, for example, I came across the contemporary writer Helen DeWitt, and couldn't stop reading her work: *The Last Samurai* (New York: Hyperion, 2000) is brilliant, gripping, moving and funny all at once; *Lightning Rods* (High Wycombe: And Other Stories, 2012) is hilarious and a risqué parody of self-help books; and, literally while I was redrafting the final chapter, I bought her new collection of different and interesting short stories, *Some Trick: Thirteen Stories* (New York: New Directions, 2018).

So I'm not going to recommend any (more) literature. There are plenty of others to do this.

Further Reading

The same sorts of problems apply to literary criticism and theory. There is a lot written and published in print and online, and some people say that the field risks being swamped by poor work. I think another risk is much, much worse: that so much wonderful, insightful material is written by so many that even a dedicated reader is going to miss a fascinating innovative interpretation of a canonical text, a thought-provoking idea about how a novel works, or a new discussion of poetics.

So here I've suggested a kind of odd, personal selection of old and new books about literature that have shaped my thinking. Although these two aspects are inextricably interwoven, and this division is simplistic, some focus more on coming to understand literature and its importance, and some focus more on how literature informs us about our world.

The Study of Literature

Derek Attridge's *The Singularity of Literature* (London: Routledge, 2004) and its sequel, *The Work of Literature* (Oxford: Oxford University Press, 2015), offer a full view of the nature of the literary and literature.

Philip Davis' *Reading and the Reader* (Oxford: Oxford University Press, 2013) has much to say about the power of literature; he also edits an accessible and important series for OUP called 'The Literary Agenda'. Rick Rylance's book in this series, *Literature and the Public Good* (Oxford: Oxford University Press, 2016), has many sensible things to say about literature and the public realm. Ben Knight's *Pedagogic Criticism:*

Reconfiguring University English Studies (Basingstoke: Palgrave Macmillan, 2017) weaves the teaching and understanding of literature together, to show how they mutually illuminate each other.

Rita Felski's *The Limits of Critique* (Chicago: University of Chicago Press, 2015) is a polemical account of where criticism is, and where it should be, as is Joseph North's *Literary Criticism: A Concise Political History* (Cambridge, MA: Harvard University Press, 2017). Rónán McDonald's edited collection *The Values of Literary Studies* (Cambridge: Cambridge University Press, 2015) is fascinating, and has a really outstanding chapter on Leavis by Simon During, called 'When Literary Criticism Mattered'. Peter Boxall's *The Value of the Novel* (Cambridge: Cambridge University, Press 2015) makes a similar case for the novel.

Sianne Ngai's *Our Aesthetic Categories: Zany, Cute, Interesting* (Cambridge, MA: Harvard University Press, 2012) is a hard read but that's because, as the title suggests, it's trying to rethink the categories we use to understand art. Peter de Bolla's *Art Matters* (Cambridge, MA: Harvard University Press, 2001) is a profound book about our responses to the aesthetic. Susanne Keen's *Empathy and the Novel* (Oxford: Oxford University Press, 2007) discusses what many take to be this key element in fiction. Caroline Levine's *Forms: Whole, Rhythm, Hierarchy, Network* (Princeton, NJ: Princeton University Press, 2015) is a new account of the significance of form.

There are two striking and clear books by Michael Wood that have much to say about literature (*Literature and the Taste of Knowledge* [Cambridge: Cambridge University Press, 2009]) and its study (*On Empson* [Princeton, NJ: Princeton University Press, 2017]).

Finally, Frank Kermode's oblique, beautiful and significant book on closure, *The Sense of an Ending*, has been reprinted (Oxford: Oxford University Press, 2000).

Literature and the World

Edward Said's work is still hugely influential in the study of literature, including his justly celebrated *Orientalism* (London: Pantheon Books, 1978) and its follow-up, *Culture and Imperialism* (London: Vintage, 1994). Paul Gilroy, especially his *Against Race: Imagining Political Culture beyond the Color Line* (Cambridge, MA: Harvard University Press, 2000) and *After Empire* (London: Routledge, 2004), refuses to duck any of the hard issues that these debates generate.

Kate Millett's *Sexual Politics* (Urbana: University of Illinois Press, 2000) and Sandra M. Gilbert and Susan Gubar's *The Madwoman in the Attic: The Woman Writer and the Nineteenth-Century Literacy Imagination* (New Haven: Yale University Press, 2000) are both extraordinary influential and have been reissued. Sara Ahmed's *Living a Feminist Life* (Durham, NC: Duke University Press, 2017) picks up some of these arguments. The work of Eve Kosofsky Sedgwick – *The Epistemology of the Closet* (Oakland: University of California Press, 2008) and *Touching Feeling: Affect, Pedagogy, Performativity* (Durham, NC: Duke University Press, 2003) – has also been inspirational.

Further Reading

Lyndsey Stonebridge's *Placeless People: Writings, Rights, and Refugees* (Oxford: Oxford University Press, 2018) links literature and the global refugee crisis.

Michael Rothberg's *Multidirectional Memory: Remembering the Holocaust in the Age of Decolonization* (Stanford: Stanford University Press, 2009) and his forthcoming *The Implicated Subject,* from the same press, cover the complex global relationship between literature and memory. Bryan Cheyette's *Diasporas of the Mind: Jewish and Postcolonial Writing and the Nightmare of History* (New Haven: Yale University Press, 2013) offers more literary readings, and Viet Thanh Nguyen's *Nothing Ever Dies: Vietnam and the Memory of War* (Cambridge, MA: Harvard University Press, 2016), through its focus on Vietnam, has a range of important things to say.

Jonathan Bate's lucid *The Song of the Earth* (London: Picador, 2001) and Ursula Heise's *Sense of Place and Sense of Planet* (Oxford: Oxford University Press, 2008) tie literature to the environment. Rob Nixon's *Slow Violence and the Environmentalism of the Poor* (Cambridge, MA: Harvard University Press, 2017) addresses the intersection between literature, global poverty and environmental destruction.

Finally, Zara Dinnen's *The Digital Banal* (New York: Columbia University Press, 2018) is one of a growing number of works which explore the impact, literary and otherwise, of the digital on our lives.

Index

120

Index

Index

Index